GW00501731

take a
vine-ripened
tomato...

Published in 1999 by
New Holland Publishers (NZ) Ltd
Auckland • Sydney • London • Cape Town

Reprinted December 1999

218 Lake Road, Northcote, Auckland, New Zealand
14 Aquatic Drive, Frenchs Forest, NSW 2086, Australia
24 Nutford Place, London W1H 6DQ, United Kingdom
80 McKenzie Street, Cape Town 8001, South Africa

Copyright © in text: Julie Biuso
Copyright © in photography: Ian Batchelor
Copyright © New Holland Publishers (NZ) Ltd

ISBN: 1-877246-14X

Managing editor: Renee Lang
Cover and design: Christine Hansen
Typesetting: M & F Whild Typesetting Services
Editor: Barbara Nielsen

Produced through Phoenix Offset, Hong Kong

All rights reserved. No part of this publication may be reproduced, stored in a retrieval system, or transmitted in any form or by any means, electronic, mechanical, photocopying, recording or otherwise, without the prior permission of the publishers and copyright holders.

take a . vine-ripened tomato...

Julie Biuso

photography by

Ian Batchelor

For my dear Luca, Ilaria and Remo,
who are far more delicious than
any recipe in this book

Acknowledgements

It's been an absolute pleasure to work with Renée Lang and Barbara Nielsen (Barbara edited my first Italian cookbook Julie Biuso Cooks Italian *in 1989, and Renée helped edit my third cookbook* Julie Biuso Cooks Vegetables *in 1991 and edited my second Italian cookbook* Julie Biuso's Italian Cooking *in 1997). I have been fortunate to be guided through this project by my friend and agent Ray Richards, and by the delightful Belinda Cooke, General Manager of New Holland New Zealand, and the dynamic Gerry Struik, founder of the New Holland group.*

On the creative team, Christine Hansen took into consideration my preference for unfiddly design and made the most of the appetite-inducing text and photography. Thankfully Ian Batchelor behaved himself this time and photographed the food (beautifully) before he ate it! Actually, the fact that he can't wait to eat my food is a compliment – he loves good food and wine as much as I do.

All the effort one makes can end in a frustrating heap if the typesetters are not 'on to it'. Fran Whild did an amazingly fast and accurate job for this book.

This has been the tightest team I have worked with on any of my books and my appreciation of everyone's skills and contributions brought to the book runs deep. Top team, guys – thanks a million.

Julie Biuso

contents

take a . vine-ripened tomato…

… a juicy red tomato, still warm from the sun. Slice it into rounds, make it glisten with a film of exquisite estate-bottled olive oil, sprinkle a few flakes of sea salt over, and a little freshly milled pepper. Load it onto a chunk of crusty sour dough bread, and stand at the kitchen sink bench to eat it, unperturbed by dribbles of juice which course in rivulets down the chin, or large crusty crumbs which fall onto the breast.

Many of my late summer lunches consist of nothing more than this, a tomato, a piece of bread and oil, eaten without ceremony at the kitchen bench as I look out on the tranquillity of my garden.

The tomato may be a recent addition to the countries of the Mediterranean, but the union of bread and oil is an old one. It has always been more important to have bread at the table than meat, and olive oil has been revered for centuries.

The Mediterranean Sea flows to the shores of three continents, each with a vastly different hinterland, but the olive tree is common to them all. Whilst the use of garlic and herbs, the souring and seasoning agents and the staple grain may vary from country to country, olive oil is the single ingredient which unites the disparate cuisines of these countries.

The olive may be the soul of Mediterranean cuisine, but the ethos of its peoples is to grow and produce food for its taste, for its nourishment, for the comfort and pleasure it brings; it is not bred for looks alone. The first bite of a piece of ripe plump fruit, washed under the tap in the marketplace and eaten in situ, is an exquisite memory many travellers carry with them for years.

In the food markets, sacks of grains and pulses, the powerhouses of the diet, vie for space on stalls with nuts and seeds and dried fruits. Cheeses, rolled in ash, wrapped in vine leaves, covered in living rind or left to soften and run over the cheese cutting board are irresistible to the cheese-lover. The colour of seasonal vegetables seems more vibrant, the perfume of fruits sweeter and more pervasive, the aromas of herbs more pungent and the fish more clear-eyed and glistening than usual. It's as if housing all this magnificent produce together accentuates its beauty. The stallholders' pride is palpable.

The depth of red in a watermelon that has been steeped in blazing sun for weeks; the sweet nectar with no hint of bitterness that dribbles from a tree-ripened peach; the surprisingly hot pungency of garlic that has no sourness; the head-turning fragrances of herbs picked before the morning sun wilts them; erect spears of asparagus, standing like guards of honour; tight-budded mauvey-green artichokes picked before the choke has a chance to form; and bulbs of fennel, crisp and white, which a mere few hours earlier were waving their feathery fronds skyward – these are attributes which are admired and sought after by the Mediterranean peoples, attributes which make the food of the region something special. Taste is everything. Dimples and bumps in fruit and vegetables are accepted; unripe or unfresh food is not.

The key to capturing the essence of this culinary melting pot is to cook seasonally, to buy the freshest food available and to consume the food as soon as possible after purchasing. *take a vine-ripened tomato…* is a collection of my favourite recipes from these sun-drenched lands. I hope you enjoy them.

mediterra
bites

Antipasti, tapas and mezes are the liberators of stuffy cocktail food, the neat rows of sameness arranged with military precision, cloying and rich or dull and tasteless, often discreetly biffed into pot plants.

Like untrained children we can pick, dip, slurp, dribble and lick fingers, taking what we want and coming back for more if the fancy takes us, in the unrestricted enjoyment of food as we tuck into tapas, munch on mezes and graze with ease.

nean

Bread, Tomatoes and Olive Oil Toast a slab of country bread, rub with a sweet sun-ripened tomato, then drizzle with delicious Catalan olive oil. Bliss.

Pa amb Tomaquet

SERVES 8

16 slices day-old coarse-textured bread
4–6 large ripe red tomatoes, halved
extra virgin olive oil, preferably from Catalonia (or at
    least use Spanish olive oil)
salt
freshly ground black pepper to taste
canned anchovy fillets or thinly sliced prosciutto
    (optional)

In an oven or on a barbecue, toast the bread on both sides until well browned. Immediately rub each side of the toast with the cut tomatoes, squeezing the tomatoes gently as you do so. This should leave a purée-like film of tomato on the toast.

Drizzle the toasts with oil, sprinkle with salt and grind on a little pepper. Serve on plates and devour using a knife and fork.

Alternatively, omit the salt and top the toast with anchovy fillets or curls of prosciutto, or Spanish ham.

Pa amb Tomaquet (bread and tomatoes) is served in many guises throughout Catalonia. Made with a textured country bread and ripe summer tomatoes it is a culinary triumph. Lightly toasted soft bread will not do, nor will watery tomatoes. If you want a stronger tomato presence, finely chop skinned and deseeded tomatoes and spread on the toasts.

How to...

Store Olive Oil — Olive oil is sensitive to light and warmth. Exposure to light soon turns it rancid, giving it an unpleasant buttery quality. Bottles of oil may look pretty on the bench but, if the oil is for consumption, it should be kept in the pantry. Dark glass bottles offer more protection than clear glass ones; oil in plastic bottles is to be avoided. Don't refrigerate olive oil because any condensation which forms on the inside of the top can fall back into the oil.

Greek Morsels Shimmering turquoise sea as clear as glass, unusual-tasting wine resinated with pine needles (some days you like it, some days you don't), delicious morsels to pick at, at any time of day or night: memories of Greece.

Dolmades with Rice

MAKES 35–40

3 tablespoons olive oil

1 large onion, very finely chopped

100g ($\frac{1}{2}$ cup) short grain rice, washed and drained

2 tablespoons pine nuts

2 tablespoons currants

2 tablespoons finely chopped parsley

1 $\frac{1}{2}$ tablespoons finely chopped mint

$\frac{1}{2}$ teaspoon salt

freshly ground black pepper to taste

400g preserved vine leaves (or use fresh vine leaves)

1 cup water mixed with the juice of 1 lemon and 3 tablespoons olive oil

Heat the oil in a frying pan and add the onion. Cook very gently until the onion is soft and lightly golden, then stir in the rice. Cook for a minute or two, stirring, then add the pine nuts, currants, parsley, mint, salt and black pepper to taste. Blend in $\frac{3}{4}$ cup of water, then cover with a lid and cook very gently for about 12 minutes, by which time the liquid should be absorbed and the rice nearly tender.

Roll and cook as described in Dolmades with Lamb and Pine Nuts (see page 18).

Greekish Salad

SERVES 6

1 teaspoon toasted ground cumin seeds (see page 27)

2 large cloves garlic, crushed

4 tablespoons extra virgin olive oil

$\frac{3}{4}$ cup black Kalamata olives, drained

thinly pared rind of $\frac{1}{2}$ lemon

1 tablespoon lemon juice

2 tablespoons chopped mint

freshly ground black pepper

1 cup pimiento-stuffed green olives, drained

1 cos lettuce, washed, drained and torn into bite-sized pieces

100g feta cheese, crumbled

Put the cumin seeds in a bowl with a crushed clove of garlic and 2 tablespoons of the oil. Add the black olives and set aside.

Put the other 2 tablespoons of oil in a small bowl and add the lemon rind, lemon juice, mint, the remaining crushed clove of garlic, plenty of black pepper and the green olives. Set aside.

When ready to assemble the salad, put the cos lettuce in a bowl and pour on both lots of olives. Toss well. Toss the feta in one of the bowls used for the olives, scatter on top, then serve the salad immediately.

Melitzanosalata

SERVES 6

2 medium eggplants
$\frac{1}{2}$ teaspoon salt
freshly ground black pepper to taste
$\frac{1}{2}$ teaspoon ground cumin
1 large clove garlic, crushed
2 tablespoons lemon juice
1 small red onion
1 medium ripe tomato, skinned
50ml extra virgin olive oil
flat leaf parsley
tomatoes, cucumber, olives and pita bread for serving

Prick the eggplants all over with a fine skewer. Sit them on the oven rack in an oven preheated to 180°C (put a piece of aluminium foil underneath to catch drips). Bake for 45–60 minutes or until they are very tender. Remove from the oven with tongs and rest them on a board. Alternatively, grill the eggplants under a hot grill or cook on a barbecue until the flesh is very tender and the skin charred.

When the eggplants are cool, slit in half with a sharp knife, then extract the flesh with a teaspoon. Transfer the flesh to a bowl and mash with a fork. Add the salt, pepper, cumin, garlic and lemon juice. Grate the onion coarsely, drain it briefly in a sieve, then add it to the bowl. Mix the ingredients well.

Dice the tomato and put in a sieve set over a bowl. Drain for 10 minutes, press to extract the juice, then mix the tomato into the eggplant

Whisk in the oil, then transfer the mixture to a small bowl. Sprinkle with a little torn parsley. Put the bowl on a serving plate and surround with wedges of tomato, slices of cucumber, olives and warm pita bread.

The melitzanosalata can be made a day ahead. Cover and chill. Blend with a fork before serving.

This makes a good choice as a nibble (it's not a dip but not quite a salad either).

Broad Bean and Feta Salad

SERVES 4

1 small red onion, sliced into rings
1kg fresh broad beans (or 500g frozen broad beans)
salt
1 tablespoon lemon juice
3 tablespoons extra virgin olive oil
1$\frac{1}{2}$ tablespoons finely chopped fresh marjoram
  (or $\frac{3}{4}$ teaspoon dried marjoram)
1 small clove garlic, crushed
freshly ground black pepper to taste
1 cup cherry tomatoes, halved if large
100g feta cheese
$\frac{1}{2}$ cup small black olives in oil, drained (optional)

Put the onion rings in a bowl and cover with cold water. Soak for 30 minutes, drain, then pat dry.

Remove the beans from their pods, then drop them into a saucepan of lightly salted boiling water. Bring the water back to the boil, then cook the beans for 5–7 minutes. If using frozen broad beans, cook for 3 minutes only, or until piping hot. Drain, refresh with cold water and drain again. When cool enough to handle, remove the tough outer skins (fiddly but essential). Set aside.

Mix together the lemon juice, oil, marjoram, garlic, black pepper and $\frac{1}{4}$ teaspoon salt to make a dressing. Put the prepared beans in a bowl and pour the dressing over. Toss well. Add the onion and tomatoes, toss again, then crumble the feta cheese over. If using the olives, arrange them on top of the salad.

Tzatziki

SERVES 8

1 large telegraph cucumber

500ml plain yoghurt

2 cloves garlic, crushed

2–3 tablespoons finely chopped mint, plus a sprig to garnish

1–2 teaspoons lemon juice (optional, depends on the sharpness of the yoghurt)

salt (optional)

sprigs of mint or slices of lemon to garnish

If the cucumber skin is tough or bitter, peel it off. If the seeds are mature, remove them. Grate the cucumber coarsely and put it in a sieve set over a bowl. Leave to drain for 30 minutes.

Line a second sieve with a piece of absorbent kitchen paper, set it over a bowl, pour in the yoghurt and leave to drain for 30 minutes.

Using your hands, squeeze out as much moisture as possible from the cucumber, then turn it into a clean bowl. Carefully transfer the yoghurt to the bowl of cucumber, peeling off the absorbent kitchen paper (use the collected whey in baking if you like).

Blend the garlic and mint into the cucumber and yoghurt, then have a taste. Add a little lemon juice to sharpen it if necessary and a few pinches of salt. Cover and refrigerate until required (tzatziki is best eaten the day it is made).

Just before serving, reblend the mixture (the yoghurt usually throws off a little more whey) and pour it into a bowl. Garnish with a few sprigs of mint or a few slices of lemon. If liked, serve with small pieces of crisp fried fish (choose a firm white fish, such as gurnard, or flathead tails, which will hold together after cooking).

There are countless versions of this cooling combination of cucumber and yoghurt. Mint is often added, making it refreshing and a good foil for spicy or fried foods. Sometimes just a hint of garlic is used, and in other recipes so much is used that the dish takes on a hot and pungent character – then the cooling yoghurt soothes its passage down the throat.

In Turkey the dish is called 'caçik' and the cucumber is usually sliced into rounds, immersed in a thin yoghurt dressing and garnished with a puddle of oil and a sprig of dill; the oil and dill are stirred in just before serving. This recipe is Greek and it is thicker than the Turkish version. A Persian recipe includes chopped hard-boiled egg, currants and dill. Whichever method you prefer, you will find it teams up perfectly with mezes of fried eggplant and zucchini, fried fish and pita bread.

This dish is easily turned into a delightful summer soup by adding more yoghurt and ice cold water.

Dolmades with Lamb and Pine Nuts

MAKES 40–50

50g butter
1 onion, finely chopped
1 large clove garlic, crushed
2 tablespoons pine nuts
$\frac{1}{4}$ teaspoon fennel seeds
$\frac{1}{2}$ teaspoon ground cumin
$\frac{1}{4}$ teaspoon ground cinnamon
100g ($\frac{1}{2}$ cup) long grain rice
400g lean minced lamb
$\frac{1}{2}$ teaspoon salt
1 cup meat stock
400–500g preserved vine leaves (or fresh vine leaves)
1 cup water mixed with the juice of 1 lemon and 3
    tablespoons olive oil

Put the butter in a large frying pan set over a low to medium heat, add the onion and cook gently until golden. Add the garlic and cook briefly, until the garlic starts to brown, then add the pine nuts, fennel seeds, ground cumin and cinnamon. Stir well and cook for 4–5 minutes. Tip in the rice, stir well, cook for 2–3 minutes more, then add the lamb mince and salt. Break up the mixture with a fork, blending well. Pour on the stock and bring to the boil. Lower the heat, cover with a lid and cook gently until the rice is nearly tender, about 12 minutes. If there is a lot of liquid left in the pan, scoop it off and discard. Cool the mixture.

Carefully separate the vine leaves under running water. Rinse well, then place them in a bowl of cold water. Plunge several leaves at a time into a large saucepan of boiling water, leave for 1–2 minutes, then remove with tongs and transfer to a bowl of cold water. When all are done, drain and shake them dry, then snip off any stems. If using fresh vine leaves, pick small, young, pale green leaves, trim and rinse well. Blanch as described, allowing 4–5 minutes cooking time, or until tender.

Place the vine leaves smooth side down on a clean bench (you'll need to do this in batches). Put a teaspoonful of filling in the middle of each leaf. Carefully fold the stem end and sides of the leaf over the stuffing, then roll up tightly, moulding the dolmades into shape (if the filling squelches out, use less stuffing).

Use any torn leaves to line a heavy-based frying pan, then put the dolmades in the pan, in one layer, seams tucked underneath; pack them in as closely as possible to prevent unrolling during cooking. Cover the top with more leaves.

Pour the water mixed with lemon juice and oil over the dolmades. Position a plate on top to hold them in place and cover with a lid. Bring to a gentle boil, then turn the heat to low and simmer very gently for about 1 hour, or until the dolmades are very tender. Remove from the heat and leave to cool (don't remove the lid). When cool, transfer to a container, cover and chill until serving time. If liked, serve a bowl of unsweetened yoghurt on the side.

Cypriot Pies Spinach with fennel seeds, grated nutmeg, crumbled feta and dill, wrapped in filo and rolled, then baked into golden flaky coils...

Spinach and Filo Pies

MAKES 12–15

1kg fresh spinach, washed well and coarsely chopped
(or 700g frozen spinach, thawed according to
instructions on packet)

$\frac{1}{4}$ cup olive oil

1 large onion, very finely chopped

125g (1 cup, crumbled) feta cheese, finely crumbled

1 tablespoon finely chopped parsley

1 tablespoon finely chopped dill

$\frac{1}{2}$ teaspoon fennel seeds

$\frac{1}{4}$ teaspoon salt

freshly ground black pepper to taste

freshly grated nutmeg to taste

375g packet (24–30 sheets) filo pastry

100g butter, melted

Put the wet spinach into a large saucepan with just the clinging water (do this in 2 batches). Cover with a lid and set over a medium heat until the spinach wilts. Drain, rinse with plenty of cold water, then leave to cool. By hand, wring out as much moisture as possible. If using frozen spinach, allow it to thaw; then wring out the moisture.

Put the oil in a frying pan and add the onion. Cook gently until soft and lightly golden, then blend the spinach in. Turn off the heat and stir in the feta, parsley, dill, fennel seeds, salt, pepper and nutmeg.

Lay the filo pastry on a clean, dry surface and keep covered with a cloth. Lift 1 sheet of filo onto a clean work surface and brush gently with melted butter. Top with another sheet of filo and brush with butter. Spread 2–3 tablespoons of the spinach mixture along one of the long edges of the pastry. Tuck in the short sides then roll up carefully into a sausage shape and curl into a coil. Transfer to a shallow buttered oven dish or tray.

Continue with the rest of the mixture, positioning the pastry coils in the dish so that they can't unfurl. Brush the tops with butter and cook in an oven preheated to 180°C, for about 20–30 minutes or until a good golden brown. Serve hot or warmish.

The pastries may be cooked ahead of time, cooled, stored at room temperature, then reheated briefly in a hot oven before serving. Alternatively, the uncooked pastries can be stored in the refrigerator, covered, for 2–3 days or, if made with fresh spinach, stored in the freezer for several months. For a change, sprinkle with sesame seeds before cooking.

Haloumi Heaven Slabs of haloumi cheese served still sizzling in the pan with a squeeze of lemon...

Sizzling Haloumi

SERVES 2–3

250g haloumi cheese
butter
1 lemon

Cut the cheese into 5mm slices and dry with absorbent kitchen paper.

Heat a non-stick frying pan over a medium heat and drop in a knob of butter. Put in the cheese and fry until lightly golden, then turn over. Squeeze a little lemon juice over the cheese and serve immediately with bread and extra lemon.

If liked, the cheese can be cooked and served in small single-serve cast iron dishes. The cast iron holds its heat, helping to keep the cheese warm and supple. Followed by a tomato or rocket salad, it makes a simple but delicious 2-minute meal.

Turkish Fritters A box grater, a mound of tight-skinned glossy zucchini, a smattering of dill, mint, and crumbled feta...

Zucchini Fritters

MAKES ABOUT 24 LARGE FRITTERS OR 40 MINI ONES

500g (6 small) zucchini
salt
3 spring onions, chopped
2 tablespoons chopped parsley
2 tablespoons chopped mint
1 tablespoon chopped dill
70g ($\frac{1}{2}$ cup) crumbled feta cheese
4 medium eggs, lightly beaten
freshly ground black pepper to taste
2 tablespoons plain flour
olive oil for frying
plain yoghurt for serving

Grate the zucchini coarsely and transfer it to a colander. Sprinkle with salt and let it drain for 30 minutes. Squeeze out moisture by hand, then wrap it in absorbent kitchen paper and dry.

Transfer the zucchini to a bowl and add the spring onions, parsley, mint, dill, feta cheese, eggs, $\frac{1}{2}$ teaspoon of salt and pepper to taste. Mix well, then blend in the flour.

Heat $\frac{1}{2}$ cup of oil in a large frying pan over a medium heat. When the oil is hot but before it starts hazing, drop tablespoonfuls of the mixture in the hot oil. Fry until golden, turn and cook the second side, then drain briefly on absorbent kitchen paper. Transfer to a serving plate and serve immediately with yoghurt.

These fritters are delightful. If you don't like dill, leave it out. If you like yoghurt, serve plenty of it as an accompaniment. If serving the fritters as small mezes, put a tiny blob of yoghurt on top of each and even a tiny mint sprig if available. The trick with the fritters is to have the mixture quite liquid with plenty of egg – this makes crisp lacy fritters, instead of gluten-bound glug when too much flour is used. Remix the batter every time you use it because the liquid quickly separates from the mass.

Top Tapas Tapir = to cover (verb) Tap = cover (noun)
No longer just a cover to keep flies out of the sherry glass. Bar-hopping in Tapas-land is a food grazer's dream.

Stuffed Red Peppers

SERVES 6–10

20 smallish elongated red peppers (capsicums)
500g old potatoes suitable for turning into a purée
salt
$\frac{1}{3}$ cup extra virgin olive oil
freshly ground black pepper to taste
2 large cloves garlic, crushed
1 medium smoked fish of your choice
olive oil
400ml cream
2 tablespoons chopped flat leaf parsley

Preheat the oven to 210°C. Put the peppers on the oven rack and cook for about 20 minutes, turning occasionally with tongs, or until they are blistered and charred. Transfer to a plate and when cool, peel off the skins and slip out the cores and seeds.

Peel the potatoes, cut into cubes, put in a saucepan and cover with cold water. Salt lightly and bring to the boil, then lower the heat and cook gently until tender. Drain the potatoes, then mash them to a purée with a potato masher. Slowly blend most of the extra virgin olive oil into the potato purée, along with $\frac{1}{4}$ teaspoon of salt, black pepper to taste and the garlic.

Take the fish off the bones, discarding skin, scales and bones, and break into large flakes. Gently blend through the potato purée.

If using elongated peppers, set aside 4 of them for the sauce. Split the rest of the peppers down a natural line in the flesh and fill with the fish mixture, folding the pepper flesh over to enclose the filling. If using squat peppers, set aside 2 for the sauce. Cut the rest of the peppers in half and place 2 tablespoons of the fish mixture on each half. Roll the pepper flesh to enclose the filling. Reserve any pepper juices. If using bottled peppers, drain them, reserving the liquid, and set aside

4 for the sauce. Stuff the whole peppers with the fish mixture.

Lay the stuffed peppers in an oiled ovenproof dish, sealed side down; pack tightly. Drizzle with olive oil and any pepper juices, then bake for 20 minutes in an oven preheated to 200°C, basting once.

Meanwhile, purée the remaining peppers in a food processor. Bring the cream to the boil in a saucepan and reduce by half over a medium heat. Stir in $\frac{1}{4}$ teaspoon of salt, black pepper to taste, the pepper purée and parsley. Spoon the sauce onto plates and top each with 2 stuffed peppers. Serve immediately. Alternatively, serve the sauce and peppers on a platter.

If smallish elongated red peppers are not available, use 10 squat red peppers, or use 20 bottled Spanish piquillo peppers (see page 24).

Use any leftover filling in any of the following ways: in a smoked fish pie; in tartlets; reheated on hot buttered toast topped with herbs, capers and roasted peppers; stuffed into hollowed-out zucchini and baked.

Traditionally, these Catalan peppers are stuffed with salt cod, a local specialty, but you may find it hard to come by and the results can be unpredictable. Should you wish to make these with salt cod, soak half an average-sized salt cod in plenty of water for 48 hours, changing the water every few hours. Gently poach the fish, remove the skin and bones and flake the flesh.

Piquillos Stuffed with Crab

SERVES 6

225g jar whole piquillo peppers (pimientos del piquillo)

50g cooked shrimps, finely chopped (remove any grey veins)

150g crab meat picked over (use fresh crab meat or buy frozen crab meat)

3 gherkins, finely chopped (pat dry on kitchen paper before chopping)

$\frac{1}{2}$ cup thick homemade mayonnaise (see opposite)

freshly ground black pepper

salt

Carefully remove the peppers from the jar, reserving any juices, and place on a plate. Mix together the shrimps, crab meat, gherkins and mayonnaise, adding a good grinding of black pepper and a sprinkling of salt. Carefully spoon into the peppers. Arrange the peppers on a plate, drizzle with the reserved juices, and serve.

Piquillo peppers are smallish beak-shaped peppers, usually sold pre-roasted and packed into jars or cans. Particularly sweet, they take on a wonderful smoky, roasted flavour from the preparation. They can be served as tapas, stuffed with various fillings, or used as a garnish. The best piquillos come from the region of Navarra, in the Pyrenees area of Spain.

Mayonnaise

3 egg yolks, at room temperature

approximately $\frac{1}{4}$ teaspoon salt

little dab of Dijon-style mustard (optional)

$1\frac{1}{4}$ cups olive oil

1–2 tablespoons white wine vinegar or lemon juice

When I make mayonnaise, I prefer to use a whisk first, then a hand-held electric beater (small quantities get lost in a food processor).

In a small bowl, mix the egg yolks, salt and mustard, if using. Use a wire whisk and beat until the yolks take on a darker colour and thicken slightly. Start whisking in the oil slowly at first, dripping it off the tines of a fork, then switch to a hand-held electric beater. Once the mixture is very thick, blend in a tablespoon of vinegar or lemon juice, then beat in the remaining oil, adding it in a thin, steady stream. Add the rest of the vinegar or lemon juice, and more salt if it tastes oily. If the mayonnaise is too thick, thin it with freshly boiled and cooled water.

I prefer to use lemon juice when the mayonnaise is to be served with fish, chicken or delicate vegetables such as asparagus.

To make garlic mayonnaise (aïoli), choose 3–4 cloves fresh young garlic. Crush the garlic with a little salt, using the back of a heavy knife, until the mixture becomes a lump-free purée. If the garlic is mature, cut the cloves open and pick out the green centre sprout (this is strong tasting and causes garlic to 'repeat'). Mix the puréed garlic with the egg yolks and seasonings. Continue as above.

Cover the surface of the mayonnaise with plastic food wrap and refrigerate until required. If fresh, healthy eggs are used, mayonnaise will keep for about a week, although I prefer to use aïoli within 1–2 days of making it, while the garlic flavour is still fresh.

Tiny Meatballs in Tomato Sherry Sauce

MAKES AT LEAST 80

2 slices stale white bread, crusts removed

500g veal and pork mince (if this is not available, straight pork mince is equally delicious)

50g prosciutto or derinded streaky bacon, chopped

salt

1 large clove garlic, crushed

grated zest of 1 lemon

$\frac{1}{4}$ teaspoon sweet paprika

freshly ground black pepper to taste

50g (about $\frac{1}{2}$ cup) pimiento-stuffed green olives, drained

2 eggs

$\frac{1}{2}$ cup plain flour

olive oil

chopped parsley and grated zest of 1 lemon to garnish

Sauce

1 onion, finely chopped

2 tablespoons olive oil

2 x 400g cans Spanish (or Italian) tomatoes (flick out as many seeds as possible)

$\frac{1}{2}$ teaspoon salt

100ml fino sherry

The meatball mixture is easily made in a food processor. Put the bread in a bowl and pour on a cup of water. Soak for 10 minutes, then wring out the water. Put the bread in the bowl of the processor, along with the mince, prosciutto or bacon, $\frac{1}{2}$ teaspoon of salt, garlic, lemon zest, paprika, black pepper and olives. Process the mixture until blended but still chunky (the olives should be coarsely chopped). Roll into small balls no bigger than a marble; the mixture should make over 80 meatballs. (Dampen your hands with water to stop the meatballs sticking to your hands as you roll them.) Put the meatballs on a tray as they are done. Chill for 1–2 hours to allow them to firm.

Put the eggs in a soup bowl and beat well with a fork, adding $\frac{1}{4}$ teaspoon of salt. Put the flour in a plastic bag. Heat $\frac{1}{4}$ cup of oil in a large non-stick frying pan. Cook the meatballs in batches as follows: coat about a dozen at a time in beaten egg, drain briefly in a sieve, them put them in the bag of flour. Shake until they are coated with flour. Cook in hot oil until golden brown, turning with 2 spoons. Add more oil if necessary, letting it reheat before adding more meatballs.

Drain the cooked meatballs briefly on crumpled absorbent kitchen paper, then add meatballs to the pan of tomato sauce (see below). When all the balls are cooked, heat them in the sauce until piping hot. Tip them into a serving dish, garnish with parsley or lemon zest and serve with a bowl of toothpicks.

Tomato Sauce

Fry the onion slowly in the oil in a saucepan until tender and a rich golden colour (don't let it burn; the temperature must be low). Tip in the tomatoes, bring to the boil, then cook gently for about 30 minutes, stirring often, or until thick and pulpy. Stir in the sherry (adding sherry to the finished sauce balances the sweet taste of the browned onions).

The meatballs and sauce can be made 24 hours before required. Cover and keep refrigerated, then reheat gently when required. The sauce makes more than you need as a dipping sauce for the balls – serve plenty of crusty bread to scoop it up.

Paella Croquettes

MAKES 10 OR MORE

1 cup leftover cooked paella rice (see page 45)

$\frac{1}{2}$ cup chopped chicken, fish or meat from a leftover paella

2 small eggs, lightly beaten

2 teaspoons plain flour

flour for dusting

dry breadcrumbs for coating (see page 69)

oil for frying

Mix the rice and chicken, fish or meat together in a bowl. Add 1 egg and the 2 teaspoons of flour. With floured hands, shape the mixture into small balls. Chill the balls for 1 hour.

Dip the balls in the second beaten egg, then in breadcrumbs. Pour oil at least 2 cm deep into a saucepan, heat and, when hot, fry the croquettes until they are golden. Drain. Serve hot or warmish.

Ensaladilla

SERVES 10–12

500g even-sized waxy salad potatoes, scrubbed

salt

2 slim carrots, cut into small dice

2 stalks white celery (use the tender stalks from the
middle of the celery), cut into small dice

$\frac{3}{4}$ cup artichokes bottled in oil, drained and sliced

1 spring onion, trimmed (white part only), finely
chopped

1 green pepper (capsicum), cored, halved, deseeded
then cut into small dice

130g diced, canned pepper (capsicum), drained, or 1
large roasted red pepper (capsicum), cored, deseeded
then cut into small dice

6 black olives, cut into slivers

2 gherkins, drained and chopped

1 $\frac{1}{2}$ tablespoons capers, drained and chopped

freshly ground black pepper

olives, strips of roasted pepper (capsicum), parsley,
sweet paprika to garnish

Mayonnaise

3 egg yolks, at room temperature

$\frac{1}{4}$ teaspoon salt

1 teaspoon Dijon-style mustard

300ml light olive oil

3 tablespoons lemon juice

Cook the potatoes in gently boiling salted water until
just tender. Drain, then peel when cool and cut into
small cubes. Put them in a large bowl.

Meanwhile, cook the carrots in gently boiling
salted water for 5 minutes. Drain, and refresh with
cold water. Tip onto a piece of absorbent kitchen paper
to dry and when cool, add to the bowl of potatoes,
along with the celery, artichoke slices, spring onion,
green pepper, diced canned pepper or roasted red
pepper, black olives, gherkins, capers, $\frac{1}{4}$ teaspoon salt
and plenty of black pepper. Mix well.

Make the mayonnaise for the salad in the normal
way (see page 24).

Mix the mayonnaise into the salad ingredients. If
you want to serve the salad immediately, pile it into a
mound on a serving plate lined with salad leaves and
garnish elaborately. Alternatively, turn the mixture
into a terrine or loaf tin, smooth the surface, wrap and
chill for 12–24 hours. To turn out, carefully loosen the
mixture from the sides of the terrine or tin with a flat-
bladed knife, cover with a long board or serving
platter, invert, then, with the aid of a knife, gently
encourage the potato mould to come out (easily done).

Garnish with any of the following: halved olives,
strips of roasted red or yellow pepper, sprigs of flat leaf
parsley, a dusting of paprika.

*This delicious salad of creamy potatoes, artichokes,
celery, carrots and pepper is given a lift with olives,
gherkins and capers. Try it as a main course with ham
off the bone or prosciutto, and a green salad. It keeps
well for 3 days, covered and refrigerated.*

Serafin's Potato Salad

SERVES 8

1kg waxy salad potatoes, scrubbed

salt

grated zest of 1 orange

2 tablespoons each orange juice and lemon juice

1 tablespoon coarsely chopped parsley

1 tablespoon chopped dill

3 tablespoons capers, drained

$\frac{1}{2}$ cup extra virgin olive oil

Position the potatoes in a metal colander or steaming
basket over a saucepan of boiling water. Sprinkle a
little salt over, then cover tightly with a lid or double
thickness of aluminium foil. Steam over vigorously
boiling water until just tender, allowing 12–15 minutes
for small potatoes and up to 30 minutes for larger
ones. Remove the colander or steaming basket from
the pot and leave the potatoes to cool slightly. Peel,
then slice into rounds and arrange in a shallow dish.

Blend the orange zest, citrus juices, parsley, dill,
capers and $\frac{1}{2}$ teaspoon of salt. Whisk in the oil. Pour
over the potatoes and marinate for at least 2 hours at
room temperature, or overnight in the refrigerator.
Serve at room temperature.

Salami Tostada

**SERVES 6 OR MORE – MAKES ABOUT 20 MINI
SANDWICHES**

olive oil

1 clove garlic, crushed

$\frac{1}{4}$ teaspoon toasted ground cumin (see opposite)

$\frac{1}{4}$ teaspoon sweet paprika

$\frac{1}{4}$ teaspoon chilli powder (optional)

100g thinly sliced mild salami, finely chopped (I prefer
   garlic sausage)

100g minced pork

1 rasher bacon, rind removed and very finely chopped

8 pimiento-stuffed green olives, chopped

1 small egg, lightly beaten

1 French loaf, sliced

softened butter

In a bowl, mix 1 tablespoon of olive oil with the garlic,
cumin, paprika and chilli powder, if using. Stir in the
salami, pork, bacon and olives and leave for 1 hour
before using.

Heat $\frac{1}{2}$ tablespoon of olive oil in a frying pan (if
using a non-stick frying pan, oil probably won't be
necessary) over a medium heat and fry the meat
mixture for 5 minutes, or until the pork and bacon are
cooked. Cool, then mix in the egg.

Spread the bread slices with butter on one side, then
make sandwiches with the bread and filling, putting the
buttered side of the bread on the outside; press them
firmly together. Cook several at a time, in a non-stick
pan or on a hot grill, over a medium heat. When they
are crisp and golden, turn them carefully and cook the
second side. As the sandwiches cook, press down on
them with a spatula, squashing them somewhat and
forcing the slices to stick together. Serve hot.

*The Spanish, so the story goes, used to cover their
drinks with a slice of stale bread to keep the wine flies
out in between sips. Some innovative bartender decided
to top the bread with a slice of ham and it was
consumed with the last mouthful of sherry. The trouble
was, the ham was salty, which meant another drink was
called for, and so the process was repeated. Tapas these
days can be as simple as an olive or chunk of chorizo,
or elaborate affairs such as layers of seafood, herbs,
olives, mayonnaise and salad on bread or pastry.*

How to...

*Toast Cumin Seeds — Toasting cumin seeds
develops a wonderfully nutty spiciness. Put the seeds in
a small, dry frying pan and set it over a medium heat.
Toast them for a few minutes, shaking the pan
occasionally until they start popping, darken in colour
and smell fragrant. Grind the seeds in a spice grinder or
pulverise them in a mortar with a pestle. When cool,
store airtight until required. Some recipes call for no
more than a teaspoon of toasted ground cumin seeds –
an impossible amount to prepare successfully. It's better
to prepare several tablespoons at a time; ground cumin
seeds will keep well for several weeks.*

Tortilla Española

SERVES 6–10

750g old potatoes
¾ cup olive oil
1 small onion, sliced
4 eggs
¾ teaspoon salt

Peel the potatoes and slice thinly. Pat dry with a clean cloth or absorbent kitchen paper.

Use a 20cm non-stick frying pan. Heat the oil in the pan over a medium heat. Slip in the potato slices, one by one, then turn the heat to low. Cover and cook for 5 minutes. Toss the potatoes carefully, then put the onion on top and continue cooking for 10 minutes, tossing often, or until the potatoes are tender but not browned. Tip the potatoes and onion into a strainer set over a bowl and drain briefly. Reserve oil.

Put the eggs and salt in a large bowl and beat until frothy. Add the drained potatoes and onion and mix in; leave for 10 minutes.

Wipe out the pan with absorbent kitchen paper and add 2 tablespoons of the drained oil. (The rest can be reused – strain it into a container, leaving the starch behind.) Heat the oil in the pan over a high heat (swirl the oil around the sides of the pan). When it is hot, tip in the egg mixture and immediately turn the heat to low. Cook gently, until a light golden brown on the underside. Place a large plate over the pan and invert the tortilla onto it. Quickly slide the tortilla back into the pan and cook the second side gently until it turns a light golden colour. Alternatively, slide the tortilla onto a large plate, cover with a second plate, invert, and slide back into the pan, uncooked side down. Serve at room temperature, cut into wedges or cubes.

This is one of those seemingly simple dishes, the sort which is easily stuffed up. The potatoes and onion need to be cooked slowly in a generous amount of oil (don't fret; 80% of it is strained off and can be reused). This gives the tortilla a particular melting quality. When the potato and egg mixture goes back into the pan, the oil must be hot, so that the egg puffs up around the sides (this prevents it sticking to the pan), but the heat must be lowered immediately so the tortilla cooks gently, keeping the inside creamy.

Tortilla is not an omelette in the French sense, but is more like an omelette-cake. The most common version is made with potatoes, but it can also be made with a variety of vegetables, and sometimes ham, and is nearly always good. Served in tapas bars all over Spain, the best tortilla I have had was in a Catalonian bar in Barcelona.

From The Souk Tempting smells of roasted cumin and ground coriander

Dukkah

$\frac{3}{4}$ cup untoasted sesame seeds

$\frac{1}{4}$ cup hazelnuts

$\frac{2}{3}$ cup coriander seeds

$\frac{1}{4}$ cup cumin seeds

$\frac{1}{4}$ teaspoon salt

freshly ground black pepper to taste

Put the sesame seeds in a shallow ovenproof dish and brown them in an oven preheated to 180°C, for 5–8 minutes until lightly golden, stirring the seeds occasionally to encourage even colouring.

Put the hazelnuts in a shallow ovenproof dish and toast them in the oven for about 12–15 minutes. The skins should burst open and the nuts should be lightly coloured. Turn the nuts into an old clean cloth, bundle up and rub them vigorously to release their outer skins.

Put the coriander seeds in a dry heavy-based frying pan. Toast them over a medium heat for 5–6 minutes until lightly toasted, swirling the seeds in the pan from time to time. Lastly, toast the cumin seeds in the same pan for about 4 minutes or until slightly darkened in colour and aromatic.

Crush the nuts and spices by hand, using the round end of a rolling pin, or grind them lightly in a food processor; don't overwork the mixture – it should be dry, not oily. Mix in the salt and black pepper.

Serve with a small dish of extra virgin olive oil and pita bread. This makes a generous quantity but left-over Dukkah will store well for several weeks if it is kept airtight.

Baba Ghannouj

SERVES 8

1 large eggplant

2 cloves garlic, crushed

$\frac{1}{2}$ teaspoon salt

$\frac{1}{4}$ cup tahini

1 $\frac{1}{2}$ tablespoons lemon juice, or to taste

$\frac{1}{4}$ cup finely chopped parsley

Pierce the eggplant with a skewer in several places to prevent it bursting, then put it under a hot grill and cook until the skin has blackened and charred and the flesh feels soft. When cool enough to handle, cut the eggplant in half and scoop out the flesh.

Alternatively, cook the pierced eggplant on an oven rack in an oven preheated to 200°C, for 45–60 minutes, turning once with tongs.

Put the eggplant flesh in a food processor. Add the garlic, salt and tahini and blend until smooth. Stop the machine, add the lemon juice and blend again. Fold the parsley through. Taste and add extra salt or lemon juice if needed.

If making by hand, blend ingredients together with a potato masher.

seeds, cinnamon, garlic and mint fill the air...

Tabbouleh

SERVES 8 OR MORE

175g (1 cup) fine burghul
3 large, ripe tomatoes, quartered, cored, and seeds
    flicked out
4 cups finely chopped parsley
2 cups tightly packed mint leaves, chopped
3 spring onions, very finely chopped
$\frac{1}{2}$ cup lemon juice
$\frac{1}{2}$ cup extra virgin olive oil
1 teaspoon salt
freshly ground black pepper to taste
lettuce leaves, olives, cucumbers and tomatoes
    to garnish

Put the burghul in a fine sieve and rinse under running water. Put it in a bowl, pour on $2\frac{1}{2}$ cups water, then leave to soak for 30 minutes. Drain well. Transfer to a large serving bowl. Dice the tomatoes and add to the bowl with the parsley, mint and spring onions.

In a small bowl, whisk together the lemon juice, oil, salt and pepper. Pour over the salad and toss well. Pile in a mound on a plate lined with lettuce leaves. Garnish with olives, sliced cucumber and tomato wedges and serve extra lettuce leaves separately for scooping up the salad.

Fresh Coriander Dressing with Cauliflower

SERVES 6 OR MORE

small bunch (about 1 cup chopped) fresh coriander,
    washed, shaken dry and roughly chopped
$1\frac{1}{2}$ teaspoons toasted ground cumin seeds (see page 27)
$\frac{1}{4}$ teaspoon salt
freshly ground black pepper to taste
few pinches ground cinnamon
100ml olive oil
$1\frac{1}{2}$ tablespoons white wine vinegar, or to taste
1 small fresh cauliflower, cut into tiny florets, washed
    and shaken dry

Put the chopped coriander, ground cumin, salt, black pepper and cinnamon into a food processor with half the oil, then process until the coriander is finely chopped.

With the machine running, pour in the rest of the oil and the vinegar and blend together. Turn into a small bowl and leave for an hour before using. When ready to serve, reblend with a fork and serve with a platter of cauliflower florets.

Coriander, cumin and cinnamon give this dressing an intriguing perfume and taste. Crisp, snow-white florets of cauliflower make the perfect dunking partner, but it also works well with steamed seafood, or crumbed and fried titbits.

Smoked Fish On Hummus Croûtes with Lemon and Mint Dressing

SERVES 6

2 x 210g cans chickpeas, drained and rinsed, or 2 cups
   cooked chickpeas

1 large clove garlic, crushed

2 tablespoons lemon juice

$\frac{1}{3}$ cup tahini

$\frac{1}{2}$ smoked fish of your choice

3 tablespoons extra virgin olive oil

$\frac{1}{4}$ teaspoon salt

1 $\frac{1}{2}$ tablespoons lemon juice

6–12 slices wholegrain or country-style bread

freshly ground black pepper to taste

2 tablespoons chopped mint

This quickly made hummus can be prepared a day in advance. Using a food processor, mix the chickpeas with the garlic, lemon juice and tahini, adding enough water to make a smooth purée. Transfer to a container, cover and chill until required.

Remove the fish from the bones, discarding skin, scales and bones. Cover and refrigerate until required. Put the oil, salt and lemon juice in a bowl for the dressing.

When ready to serve, toast the bread, spread generously with hummus and slice into fingers or triangles. Top with the smoked fish and grind on a little black pepper. Blend the dressing, adding mint. Drizzle over the toasts then serve immediately.

Crispy Garlic Pita Breads

75g butter, softened

2 cloves garlic, crushed

4–6 large pita breads

Put the butter in a bowl and beat in the garlic. Snip the pita breads in half horizontally with scissors and spread the insides of them with butter.

Arrange the pita breads, buttered side up, in a shallow roasting tin and bake for 8–10 minutes, until crispy and lightly golden, in an oven preheated to 180°C (cook them in batches). Cool, then store in an airtight container.

The pita breads store well for 2–3 days.

Smoked Fish On Hummus Croûtes with Lemon and Mint Dressing

Spiced Hummus with Golden Onion Topping

SERVES 8

2 cups dried chickpeas, soaked 24 hours in cold water
   (or use 4 cups canned chickpeas, rinsed and drained)

3 tablespoons lemon juice

3 tablespoons tahini

2 cloves garlic, crushed

$\frac{1}{2}$ teaspoon ground cumin

salt

2 large onions, sliced

75ml olive oil

$\frac{1}{4}$ teaspoon chilli powder

$\frac{1}{2}$ teaspoon freshly ground coriander seeds

$\frac{1}{2}$ teaspoon ground cumin

1 tablespoon finely chopped mint

A sneaky hit of chilli in the sweet caramelized onion and mint topping on this creamy hummus wakes up the taste buds. Serve it with warmed, puffy pita bread, or Crispy Garlic Pita Bread (see page 33). To turn it into a more substantial snack, serve it with rounds of barbecued eggplant, sticks of peeled crisp cucumber, lemon wedges and a bowl of olives.

Drain the chickpeas, transfer them to a saucepan and cover generously with cold water. Bring to the boil and cook at a fast boil for 10 minutes. Skim well, then lower the heat, partially cover with a lid and cook at a gentle boil for about 1 hour, or until very tender (this can take 2–3 hours – don't be surprised!). Drain, reserving some liquid. If you can be bothered to skin the chickpeas, the hummus will be much creamier and more luxurious.

Transfer the chickpeas to the bowl of a food processor and add the lemon juice, tahini, garlic, cumin and $\frac{3}{4}$ teaspoon of salt. Blend until smooth, then taste, adding some more lemon juice or salt if needed, and a little of the thickened cooking water if the purée is too stiff.

Put the onions in a large frying pan with the oil and cook gently for about 30 minutes, stirring often, until they are a rich golden colour. When cooked, drain off most of the oil, add the chilli powder, coriander and the second measure of cumin and $\frac{1}{4}$ teaspoon of salt, then cook for another 2 minutes.

Turn the hummus into a shallow bowl and pour the contents of the frying pan over the top. Sprinkle with mint and serve immediately.

A Honey of a Recipe Cooking eggplants in my kitchen North African–style with Claudia Roden seemed like a dream...

Claudia's Honeyed Eggplant

SERVES 6–8

750g (about 3 small) eggplants

salt

2–3 garlic cloves, crushed

sunflower oil for frying

5cm piece ginger, grated, or the juice squeezed out in a garlic press

1 teaspoon ground cumin

a large pinch of cayenne or chilli pepper, or to taste

5 tablespoons runny honey

juice of 1 lemon

Remove the calyx and stem from each eggplant, then cut eggplants into 1cm slices. Sprinkle generously with salt and leave in a colander for one hour to release their juices, then wash off the salt and dry them with absorbent kitchen paper.

Prepare the honey sauce. In a wide frying pan, fry the garlic in 2 tablespoons of oil for seconds only, stirring until the aroma rises, then take it off the heat; do not let it brown. Add the ginger, cumin and cayenne or chilli pepper, the honey and lemon juice and about 5 tablespoons of water.

Fry the eggplant slices in a separate frying pan in very hot oil, turning them over once, until they are lightly browned. They do not need to be thoroughly cooked as they will cook further in the sauce. Drain them on absorbent kitchen paper and gently press more paper on top to remove as much oil as possible.

Now cook the eggplant slices in the honey sauce over a low heat, either in batches so that they are in one layer, or put them all in together and rearrange them so that each gets some cooking in the sauce. Cook for about 10 minutes, or until the slices have absorbed the sauce and become soft; add a little water if necessary.

Let cool and serve cold or at room temperature with bread.

These are Claudia's tips:

If the eggplants are large, they can be cut into rounds, then halves.

Oil the spoon before dipping it into the honey so the honey doesn't stick to the spoon.

If the mixture dries up in the pan when cooking the eggplants, add a little water.

For this North African dish, Claudia uses small eggplants and orange blossom honey, but suggests you can use any scented honey and quite a bit of chilli pepper. Believe me, she knows what she's talking about.

How to...

Oven-bake Eggplant Fried eggplant is rich and delicious to eat, but it has a bad habit of soaking up too much oil. If the eggplant is to be incorporated into other dishes, or when you want a less rich dish, it can be brushed with olive oil and oven-baked. This uses much less oil than frying and ensures the dish it is incorporated into does not become excessively rich and oily.

Slice the eggplant into rounds and brush both sides with olive oil. Lay the slices flat in 1 layer on a baking tray (line the tray with a teflon sheet if you have one). Bake for about 20 minutes, or until tender and brown, in an oven preheated to 180°C. Use immediately, or cool, refrigerate and use within 24 hours.

when comes

Springtime.

Season of new life. Warmer air.

Tender shoots. Peas, broad beans, artichokes, asparagus, fennel bulbs, young salad greens and herbs, strawberries, baby lamb. Enjoy them in season.

spring

A VERDANT TREAT FROM MOROCCO
Moroccan Broad Bean Purée
Roasted Tomatoes

THE ESSENCE OF SPRING
Prawn, Asparagus and Broad Bean Salad
Pasta Shells with Broad Bean and Bacon Sauce
Broad Bean Salad with Mint

SPANISH RICE
Vegetarian Paella

NOUVEAU GREEK
Roasted Asparagus and Yellow Peppers with Marinated Feta

CRISP AND GOLDEN
Chicken in Crispy Prosciutto

DIVINE LAMB
Lamb in Vine Leaves

BUTTERFLIES AND ARTICHOKES
Farfalle with Roasted Artichokes
Roasted Artichokes, Prosciutto and Parmigiano
Penne with Garlic, Oil and Rocket

A Verdant Treat From Morocco ...And there were bowls of a thick verdant purée, shimmering with oil, speckled with paprika – 'bissara' the locals called it.

Moroccan Broad Bean Purée

SERVES 6–8 AS A NIBBLE

1kg fresh broad beans or 500g frozen broad beans
salt
$1\frac{1}{2}$ tablespoons lemon juice
1 large clove garlic, chopped
1 small green chilli, deseeded and chopped
50ml extra virgin olive oil
sweet paprika for dusting

Prepare the broad beans first. If fresh, remove them from their pods and drop them into a saucepan of lightly salted boiling water. Return to the boil and cook for 10 minutes, or until tender. Drain and refresh with cold water. If using frozen broad beans, cook in the same manner, but for 3 minutes only once the water returns to the boil. Next, remove the beans from their skins (fiddly but necessary). Transfer the beans to the bowl of a food processor.

Add the lemon juice, $\frac{1}{4}$ teaspoon of salt, the garlic, chilli and most of the oil. Process until smooth. Transfer to a bowl, make a small hollow in the purée and fill with oil. Dust with a little paprika and serve with Roasted Tomatoes (see opposite). The purée can be made a day ahead; cover and chill.

Bissara can form the basis of a casual lunch or light meal (serves 4). Spread the bissara on chunks of crusty bread or toasted focaccia, or use pita pockets, and top with Roasted Tomatoes. Accompany with a bowl of olives and a handful of baby salad greens and coriander leaves dressed with lemon, extra virgin olive oil, salt, pepper and crushed garlic.

Roasted Tomatoes

SERVES 6–8

8 large plum-shaped Roma tomatoes, halved
$\frac{1}{2}$ teaspoon salt
1 teaspoon castor sugar
freshly ground black pepper
several sprigs fresh thyme
1 tablespoon extra virgin olive oil

Put the tomatoes cut side facing up in a shallow non-stick ovenproof tin (a Swiss roll tin is ideal; if it is not non-stick, line it with baking paper).

Sprinkle the salt and sugar over, grind on some pepper and scatter the thyme leaves on top (discard the stalks). Drizzle the tomatoes with the oil, then bake for $1\frac{1}{2}$ hours in an oven preheated to 170°C.

Cool before serving. The tomatoes can be prepared a day in advance; keep covered and refrigerated.

The Essence of Spring
Baby broad beans, in the flush of youth, dazzle like emeralds atop a salad of mint leaves and salty ham splashed with sherry vinegar. They nestle into pasta shells swathed in a creamy bacon sauce and tangle with crisp asparagus and pink prawns on a light seasonal salad.

Prawn, Asparagus and Broad Bean Salad

SERVES 4 AS A LIGHT MAIN COURSE, OR 6 AS A STARTER

500g fresh broad beans (or 250g frozen broad beans)

salt

12 green king prawns

12 asparagus spears, trimmed

1 curly endive lettuce, separated into leaves, washed and dried

1 tablespoon lemon juice

3 tablespoons extra virgin olive oil

1 clove garlic, crushed

6 spring onions, trimmed and cut into short lengths

grated zest of 1 lemon

freshly ground black pepper to taste

2 tablespoons chopped chervil

Prepare the beans as described in Moroccan Broad Bean Purée (see page 40). Set aside.

Twist the heads off the prawns and peel away the shells. Slit down the back of each prawn with a sharp knife and gently extract the black or orangey-red veins running down the length. Rinse and pat dry with absorbent kitchen paper.

Plunge the asparagus spears into a saucepan of lightly salted boiling water and cook for 2–5 minutes, depending on thickness. Drain, refresh with cold water, then pat dry with absorbent kitchen paper.

Put the endive leaves in a large salad bowl, sprinkle on a scant $\frac{1}{4}$ teaspoon of salt, the lemon juice and 2 tablespoons of the oil. Arrange the beans and halved asparagus spears on top of the endive.

Put the last tablespoon of oil in a frying pan, set over a low to medium heat and add the garlic and spring onions. Cook for 3–4 minutes, or until the spring onions are partially cooked. Increase the heat to medium-high and add the prawns. Cook briefly, until the prawns are pink and just cooked through. Sprinkle the lemon zest on, grind on plenty of black pepper, mix in the chervil, then tip the contents of the pan on top of the salad. Toss lightly. Serve immediately.

Pasta Shells with Broad Bean and Bacon Sauce

SERVES 4–6

1kg (generous) fresh broad beans (or 500g frozen
    broad beans)
salt
1 tablespoon olive oil
2 knobs butter
1 large onion, finely chopped
1 large clove garlic, crushed
125g streaky bacon, derinded and finely chopped
1 teaspoon finely chopped marjoram
freshly ground black pepper to taste
2 tablespoons white wine
300ml cream
400g conchiglie (pasta shells)
freshly grated Italian parmesan cheese for serving

Prepare the beans as described in Moroccan Broad Bean Purée (see page 40). Set aside. Put the oil and butter in a frying pan over a low to medium heat. Add the onion, garlic and bacon and cook until lightly golden. Sprinkle the marjoram over and grind on plenty of black pepper. Stir well, then add the wine and allow to evaporate for 3–4 minutes. Add the beans and pour in the cream, then bubble up for 2–3 minutes only, until the mixture just starts to thicken (if the pasta is not ready, turn off the heat and cover the sauce with a lid).

Meanwhile, cook the pasta in plenty of gently boiling well-salted water until al dente. Drain well. Turn into a large heated bowl and pour the sauce over. Toss quickly, then serve immediately with grated parmesan cheese.

Broad Bean Salad with Mint

SERVES 8

2kg fresh broad beans (or 2 x 500g packs frozen
    broad beans)
6 leafy stalks fresh mint leaves
salt
120g prosciutto, chopped
$\frac{1}{2}$ cos lettuce, washed, dried and chopped
$1\frac{1}{2}$ tablespoons sherry vinegar
freshly ground black pepper to taste
1 teaspoon Dijon-style mustard
4 tablespoons extra virgin olive oil

Prepare the beans as described in Moroccan Broad Bean Purée (see page 40), adding the mint stalks, but not the leaves, to the water.

Transfer the beans to a large bowl and add the prosciutto and lettuce. In a small bowl, mix the vinegar, $\frac{1}{4}$ teaspoon of salt, pepper and mustard. Blend in the oil. Chop the mint and add to the dressing. Pour over the bean salad, toss gently and serve immediately.

Paella is the most widely travelled dish of Spain. Essentially a rice dish, it may or may not contain seafood. Search out Spanish rice.

Use either a 36cm paella dish, or a large enamelled ovenproof dish (incorrectly called a paella dish). Failing this, start the paella in a large heavy-based frying pan but, once you have mixed the rice with the seasonings, divide it between 2 heavy-based frying pans and do all the cooking on the stove top (have extra hot stock on hand in case it evaporates before the vegetables and rice are tender). The idea is to give ingredients the broadest possible surface so that liquid evaporates quickly.

Spanish Rice... Splash with Tio Pepe, infuse for 5 minutes, then lift off the covering and drink in the sweet aromatic fragrance. Grains of rice, plumped with delicious juices from spring vegetables – this is the beauty of an all–vegetable paella.

Vegetarian Paella

SERVES 10

100g dried chickpeas, soaked overnight in cold water, (or use 300g canned chickpeas)

1kg fresh broad beans, or 500g frozen broad beans

salt

$\frac{1}{2}$ cup Spanish extra virgin olive oil

1 large onion, finely chopped

12 shallots, peeled

4 cloves garlic, crushed

1 $\frac{1}{2}$ teaspoons sweet paprika

3 cups Spanish rice

6 cups vegetable or chicken stock (see page 59)

$\frac{1}{2}$ cup dry white wine

$\frac{1}{2}$ teaspoon saffron strands soaked in 2 tablespoons warm water

grated zest of 1 lemon

1 tablespoon lemon juice

4 fresh bay leaves

3 tablespoons chopped parsley

4 small fennel bulbs, trimmed and quartered

$\frac{3}{4}$ cup frozen baby peas

freshly ground black pepper to taste

275g jar artichoke hearts in olive oil, drained and halved

Tio Pepe sherry (optional)

Put the drained chickpeas in a saucepan with cold water to cover. Bring to the boil and cook at a fast boil for 10 minutes, then drain and rinse. Cover with fresh water, bring to the boil, then skim well and lower the heat. Partially cover with a lid, and cook at a gentle boil for about 1 hour, or until very tender (this can take 2–3 hours – don't be surprised!). Drain; when cool, flick off loose skins.

If the broad beans are fresh, remove them from their pods, and drop the beans into a saucepan of lightly salted boiling water. Return to the boil and cook for 5–8 minutes, until just tender. Drain and refresh with cold water. If using frozen broad beans, cook in the same way, but drain immediately after the water comes back to the boil. Remove the beans from their tough outer skins as soon as they are cool enough to handle (fiddly but necessary). Put the beans in a covered container and refrigerate.

Both the chickpeas and broad beans can be prepared the day before making the paella.

Heat a paella dish over a medium heat and add the oil. When it is hot, add the onion, shallots and garlic. Sauté gently for about 20 minutes until the onion is wilted and lightly golden. Add the paprika and rice, and stir well to coat the rice with the flavourings. The paella can be prepared several hours ahead to this point (and I think it is better for it, as the flavours permeate the rice).

Bring the stock to boiling point. Reheat the rice mixture if necessary. Stir 4 cups of the stock into the rice, add the wine, soaked saffron, lemon zest and juice, bay leaves, most of the parsley, the fennel and peas. Add 1 $\frac{1}{4}$ teaspoons of salt and grind on plenty of black pepper. Bring to the boil and cook, uncovered, stirring occasionally, over a medium heat for about 10 minutes or until most of the liquid has evaporated (the mixture should still be sloppy).

Pour in the rest of the stock and add the broad beans, chickpeas and artichoke hearts. Bring back to the boil and transfer the paella to an oven preheated to 170°C and cook for 10 minutes, or until the rice is tender (be careful not to dry it out; add a few tablespoons of hot water if it is not yet cooked).

Remove the paella from the oven, splash with Tio Pepe if using, and drape loosely with aluminium foil. Leave it to infuse for 5 minutes, sprinkle with remaining parsley then serve from the dish.

In my opinion, paella served warmish has more flavour than when it is piping hot.

Nouveau Greek The Greeks have been making feta for centuries but there's no law to say that the only salad it can grace is the classic Greek one.

Roasted Asparagus and Yellow Peppers with Marinated Feta

SERVES 6 AS A STARTER

2 large yellow peppers (capsicums), halved, cored and
    deseeded

extra virgin olive oil

salt

freshly ground black pepper to taste

400g asparagus spears, trimmed and washed

Balsamic Dressing

3 tablespoons extra virgin olive oil

1 tablespoon balsamic vinegar

$\frac{1}{4}$ teaspoon salt

1 clove garlic, crushed

1 endive lettuce, washed and dried

180g marinated feta cheese

Cut the peppers into chunks and put them in a shallow ovenproof dish. Drizzle a little oil over, sprinkle with salt and grind on some pepper. Cook for 10–15 minutes or until browned, in an oven preheated to 200°C. Alternatively, chargrill the pepper chunks on a barbecue hot plate.

Put the asparagus in a shallow roasting tin, drizzle on a little oil and sprinkle with salt. Cook in an oven preheated to 220°C for about 12 minutes, or until lightly browned.

Whisk the dressing ingredients together in a bowl. Distribute the endive among 6 plates and arrange the cheese, peppers and asparagus on top. Rewhisk the dressing and spoon over. Serve immediately.

Roasting asparagus sounds an odd thing to do – until you try it. It produces deliciously nutty-tasting spears with a faint caramel taste. Thin spears will become golden and crisp; fatter spears will turn crisp on the tips and be wonderfully juicy – take your pick!

If marinated feta is not available, use fresh feta cheese, or marinate fresh feta cheese in olive oil, garlic and herbs for 2–3 days.

Roasted Asparagus and Yellow Peppers with Marinated Feta

Crisp and Golden Take plump chicken breasts, smear them with tarragon-flavoured garlic butter, roll up in prosciutto and bake until the prosciutto is curling up in irresistible golden crisps. Yum!

Chicken in Crispy Prosciutto

SERVES 4

50g butter, softened

$\frac{1}{4}$ teaspoon salt

freshly ground black pepper

4 cloves garlic, crushed

2 tablespoons chopped fresh tarragon (if fresh tarragon is not available, use 1 tablespoon dried tarragon)

12 boned chicken thigh fillets, skinned and visible fat removed (try to choose even-sized thighs)

250g thinly sliced prosciutto

600g spinach

grated nutmeg

Mix most of the butter, the salt, pepper, garlic and tarragon in a small bowl. Spread over the insides of the chicken thighs. Roll up each thigh, then wrap tightly in prosciutto. Put the chicken thighs in a shallow ovenproof dish (a Swiss roll tin is ideal) and bake for 15 minutes in a hot oven preheated to 190°C, or until just cooked.

A certain amount of judgment is required to cook the chicken thighs to perfection. How long they take to cook depends on the size of the thighs (they vary enormously) and the oven temperature. If they cook gently, which will keep them moist, the prosciutto will not become crisp; remove the chicken thighs from the oven, heat the grill, pour off any juices and grill the chicken until the prosciutto is crisp.

Meanwhile, heat a large frying pan over a high heat, drop in the remaining knob of butter and let it sizzle and brown. Add the washed spinach leaves and cook for a few minutes until they are wilted, turning with tongs, then season with salt, pepper and grated nutmeg. Tilt the pan to drain, then arrange the spinach on individual plates and top with the sliced chicken thighs. Serve hot.

How to...

Use Garlic — If garlic is stored in a moist or warm place, it will start to sprout. The green sprout is strong tasting and is the culprit, I believe, for garlic 'repeating' on you later. It is easily removed by cutting the garlic in half and picking out the sprout with the point of a sharp knife. Old and yellowing garlic should be thrown out; it will taste sour and can ruin a dish, especially if used raw.

Garlic is at its strongest when used raw. When it is crushed, a chemical reaction takes place as the cells are broken down. The crushed paste or juice is very potent. If you want less of a hot bite from garlic, chop it, or if you prefer it milder, slice it.

Divine Lamb Juicy lamb steaks topped with caramelized onion, tomato, slabs of feta and sprigs of mint, wrapped in vine leaves and baked. There's no more fitting word than divine!

Lamb in Vine Leaves

SERVES 4–6

vine leaves (packed in brine or salt, or fresh)

2 tablespoons olive oil (approximately)

6 flank, topside, or trim lamb steaks, 2cm thick,
    trimmed of fat

2 medium onions, thinly sliced

2 cloves garlic, crushed

salt

freshly ground black pepper to taste

2–3 medium tomatoes, skinned and sliced (choose
    fleshy tomatoes, not watery ones)

175g feta cheese, cut into 6 slabs (choose a dry feta,
    not a soft moist one)

mint leaves

First prepare the vine leaves. If the vine leaves are in brine or packed in salt, immerse them in a large bowl of cold water. Separate the leaves carefully in the water, then drain the bowl and refill it with fresh water. Repeat this several times, until all traces of salt or brine are washed off. The leaves are then ready to use.

If you are using fresh leaves, pick large new leaves (usually paler in colour). Rinse them well, then poach several at a time in simmering water, until they change colour and become limp (about a minute). Drain and rinse, then hold in water until required.

Heat the oil in a large heavy-based frying pan over a medium-high heat until quite hot. Quickly sear the steaks until lightly browned, turning them with tongs. Transfer the steaks to a cake rack set over a plate. Leave to drain and cool.

Lower the heat under the pan and add the onions and garlic (add a little more oil if the pan is dry). Fry gently, stirring often, until a rich golden colour – about 15 minutes.

Drain the water from the vine leaves and give them a good shake. Spread them out on a clean work bench, using 2 large leaves for each steak. Lay the steaks on the leaves and sprinkle generously with salt and black pepper. Top with a spoonful of onion, a few slices of tomato, a slab of feta and several mint leaves.

Fold the sides of the vine leaves over the meat, then wrap into a parcel shape. Wrap in aluminium foil then put the parcels on a baking tray. Cook in an oven preheated to 200°C for 15 minutes, then carefully remove the foil, transfer the steaks to a serving plate and serve immediately.

Butterflies and Artichokes

Sometimes a little indulgence is worth its weight in gold. A small but expensive jar of comestibles, an exquisite little morsel, a titbit, a tad of that, and voilà! 5-minute wonders can emerge from the kitchen.

Farfalle with Roasted Artichokes

SERVES 4

280–300g jar charcoal-roasted or grilled artichokes in olive oil
400g farfalle (pasta butterflies)
salt
½ cup freshly grated Italian parmesan cheese, plus extra for serving
freshly ground black pepper to taste

Drain the artichokes in a sieve set over a bowl (reserve the oil), then slice them thinly.

Cook the pasta in plenty of gently boiling, well-salted water until al dente. Drain and turn into a heated serving bowl. Pour the reserved artichoke oil over, toss well, then sprinkle the cheese, a few pinches of salt and the sliced artichokes over the pasta. Grind on some pepper and toss well. Serve immediately with extra parmesan cheese.

Roasted Artichokes, Prosciutto and Parmigiano

SERVES 6–8

280–300g jar charcoal-roasted or grilled artichokes in olive oil
200g thinly sliced prosciutto
small wedge Italian parmesan cheese

Drain the artichokes in a sieve set over a bowl (reserve the oil), then slice into thick wedges. Arrange on a platter or on individual plates with the slices of prosciutto. Shave the parmesan cheese into curls with a vegetable peeler, letting it fall on the plate on top of the prosciutto and artichokes as you prepare it. Pour a little of the reserved oil over. Serve immediately with crunchy bread.

Penne with Garlic, Oil and Rocket

SERVES 4

250g rocket leaves, trimmed (approximately 4–5 packed cups of leaves)
400g penne (quill-shaped pasta)
salt
½ cup extra virgin olive oil
4 large cloves garlic, sliced
1 ½ tablespoons chilli flakes (or use 3–4 tiny dried 'bird's eye' chillies, crushed)
freshly grated Italian parmesan cheese for serving

Wash the rocket leaves, shake dry and chop coarsely.

Cook the pasta in plenty of gently boiling, well-salted water until al dente.

Meanwhile, put the oil in a small frying pan and set over a medium heat. Add the garlic and chilli flakes and ¼ teaspoon of salt. Cook gently until the garlic colours lightly. Immediately take the pan off the heat.

Drain the pasta and tip into a generous-sized heated serving bowl. Tip in all the contents of the pan (use a scraper) and scatter the rocket on top.

Toss vigorously, then serve immediately with plenty of parmesan cheese.

quintes
summer

Nothing reminds
me more of summer than lemons.
Is it the colour? No, it's memories of lying on prickly
grass with my sisters in the 1960s, listening to
the transistor radio ('Yellow Polka Dot
Bikini') and sipping icy-cold freshly squeezed
lemon drinks with floating leaves of mint that
always blocked the straws. The scent of lemons evokes the
feeling of those lazy summer days, still
fresh in my memory.

sential

A Chill Thrill In sweltering heat nothing beats a bowl of icy well-seasoned summer vegetables, blended to a palatable pulp, and sharpened with the haunting aroma and sharp tang of aged sherry vinegar. As the icy-cold pungent liquid flows down the throat, it excites and invigorates. It's the ultimate refreshing teaser for the courses to come.

Gazpacho

SERVES 8

1 red onion

2 slices stale, coarse-textured bread

2 cucumbers (I prefer telegraph cucumbers)

600g canned Spanish tomatoes (or more for a thinner soup)

3 large cloves garlic, chopped (remove any greenish sprouts)

$\frac{1}{4}$ teaspoon cayenne pepper

2 teaspoons salt

3 tablespoons extra virgin olive oil

2 large red peppers (capsicums), halved, seeded, cored and finely chopped

2 tablespoons sherry or red wine vinegar

Slice the onion finely, put it in a bowl and pour on cold water to cover; soak for 15 minutes.

Put the bread slices in a shallow dish, cover with cold water and soak for 15 minutes.

Peel the cucumbers, then cut them in half lengthways and scoop out the seeds with a teaspoon. Chop the flesh coarsely.

Put the tomatoes in a bowl and scoop out as many seeds as possible (easily done with a small teaspoon).

Drain the onion and put it in the bowl of a food processor with the garlic, cayenne pepper, salt and oil. Squeeze the excess water out of the bread and add to the processor bowl. Blend until smooth. Add the red peppers and vinegar and blend again until smooth. Transfer to a jug or bowl. Put the cucumbers and one-third of the tomatoes in the processor and process until very smooth. Add the rest of the tomatoes and process until blended. Mix with the other ingredients in the jug or bowl.

Blend in 1 cup of water, then chill the gazpacho for several hours; check the seasoning – it may need more salt or vinegar. About 45 minutes before serving, put the gazpacho in the freezer. Serve icy cold, ladled into small chilled bowls. If liked, serve with a bowl of tiny croûtons made from coarse-textured bread, and small bowls of chopped onion, pepper, cucumber and tomato.

Although it's not traditional, topping each bowl with a sliver or two of avocado, and basil or coriander leaves makes an interesting change. And if you really want to think outside the square, serve with a bowl of partially shelled prawns fried in garlic oil (dunk them in the gazpacho and eat with your fingers!).

The word 'gazpacho' means 'soaked bread' in Arabic. The Romans established bread baking when they first came to Spain and many Spanish dishes use bread as a thickener. The bread was pounded with olive oil and water until an amalgam was formed. The presence of vinegar is yet another Roman link. It makes you sweat, and sweating cools the body. Salt in the soup replaces the salt lost through sweating. A perfect recipe for hot weather.

There are many variations. Later, tomatoes were added, and these days cucumber and peppers are usually part of what we know as gazpacho. When tomatoes are at their peak, in late summer, use them (peeled) in place of canned tomatoes.

Gazpacho can be a thin watery soup – the Greeks and Romans wrote about it as a drinkable food. There might not be any bread in the soup, but croûtons, along with other chopped salad ingredients, might be served separately. The soup can be a purée or coarse textured. Further inland, gazpacho can turn up as a hot soup of seafood or game, and around Malaga gazpacho can be a chilled white soup made with almonds and grapes!

Serve chilled gazpacho icy cold, because it will warm quickly at room temperature. Chill the bowls and serve them embedded in larger bowls of ice. Alternatively, serve it thin and icy, in chilled shot glasses, as a welcome drink to guests.

The Scent of Lemons Lemon is the true thirst quencher and is welcome in any summer dish. A few squirts bring a burst of freshness, a little lip-puckering...

Moroccan Chicken with Lemon and Olives

SERVES 4–6

1 chicken, cut into 8 pieces

3 tablespoons olive oil

$\frac{3}{4}$ teaspoon salt

freshly ground black pepper to taste

1 large onion, finely chopped

2 cloves garlic, crushed

2 teaspoons sweet paprika

1 teaspoon ground ginger

1 teaspoon ground cumin

$\frac{1}{2}$ preserved lemon, rinsed; use peel only and cut into
   long strips (flesh is discarded)

juice of 1 lemon

$\frac{1}{2}$ cup chopped coriander

1–2 cups pimiento-stuffed green olives

Remove as much skin and fat from the chicken joints as possible. Brown the chicken in 2 tablespoons of the oil in a frying pan over a medium heat; cook in batches if necessary. Transfer the chicken joints to a plate once they are cooked and drain briefly. Transfer them to a casserole, sprinkle with the salt and grind on some black pepper.

Add the last tablespoon of oil to the frying pan with the onion. Cook gently until softened and browned then add the garlic and spices and cook for a few minutes more, stirring. Pour in 1 cup of water, bring to the boil and reduce briefly. Pour the mixture over the chicken, set the casserole over heat and bring to the boil again. Put on a lid and cook very gently for about 30 minutes.

Add the preserved lemon peel, lemon juice, coriander and olives. Cook for a further 20 minutes, or until the chicken is very tender. Let the chicken cool in the casserole, still covered with the lid, for 15 minutes, then transfer the chicken joints to a serving bowl; cover them loosely with aluminium foil. Set the casserole back on a medium heat and reduce the juices. Pour over the chicken and serve warmish.

Use the chicken back to make stock, then freeze the stock until required, or freeze the chicken back until it is convenient to make stock. If preferred, buy chicken joints instead of a whole chicken.

Lemon Potatoes

SERVES 6–8

1.5kg potatoes, peeled and cut into long fingers

1 teaspoon dried oregano, preferably Greek

$\frac{1}{2}$ teaspoon salt

freshly ground black pepper to taste

$\frac{1}{3}$ cup olive oil

juice of 2 lemons

Put the potato fingers in a large roasting tin with $\frac{1}{4}$ cup of water. Sprinkle the oregano and salt over, then grind on some pepper and drizzle with oil.

Put in an oven preheated to 200°C and cook for 45 minutes, turning once or twice. Pour the lemon juice over and continue cooking for 20–30 minutes more, or until crunchy.

Transfer to a serving dish. Serve hot or warmish, as a nibble, or as an accompaniment to other dishes.

If you've been to Greece, you'll have eaten heaps of these crisp and oily potatoes squirted with fresh lemon juice. I have successfully cooked old roasting potatoes and freshly dug pink-skinned waxy potatoes (Desirée) by this method.

Greek Roast Chicken

SERVES 4

1 roasting chicken

1 teaspoon dried Greek rigani or Sicilian oregano (if not available use fresh marjoram)

Maldon sea salt

freshly ground black pepper to taste

$\frac{1}{2}$ lemon, cut in 2 pieces

4 large cloves garlic (or more, to taste), peeled

2 tablespoons extra virgin olive oil

6 medium roasting potatoes, peeled and cut into chunks

lemon and fresh oregano to garnish

Cut the chicken all the way down each side of the backbone with a pair of scissors or poultry shears and force it to lie flat (snap the thigh and wing ball and socket joints). Rinse the chicken and pat dry with absorbent kitchen paper. Sprinkle the inside of the chicken with most of the oregano and a little salt and grind on a little black pepper. Transfer it to a rack set over a roasting tin (use a smallish cake rack set in a large roasting tin), turning it skin side up. Use the chicken back as described on page 57.

Rub the lemon pieces over the chicken skin. Cut 1 clove of garlic into 4 slivers and insert between the breast skin and breast meat. Sprinkle the chicken skin with oregano and some more salt and grind on black pepper, then drizzle the oil over.

Cook the chicken in an oven preheated to 200°C for 45 minutes, basting twice. Put the potatoes and the remaining garlic cloves, halved, in the juices around the chicken and roast for 35–45 minutes more, basting the chicken and turning the potatoes in the juices. When the garlic cloves are done, transfer them to a warmed plate.

When the chicken is well-browned and cooked through, transfer it to a board but continue cooking the potatoes until they are golden and tender (don't cover the chicken). Serve the chicken, potatoes and garlic on a heated serving plate. Break the chicken into serving pieces using a knife and fork. Garnish with slivers of lemon and fresh oregano. Squeeze on a little lemon juice before serving.

Chicken Stock

Chicken stock is easy to make and adds goodness to soups, sauces and gravies. Use the carcass from a roast chicken (make the stock the day after roasting the chicken) and freeze until required.

cooked chicken carcass, bones and skin

1 carrot, quartered

2 sticks celery, chopped into short lengths

1 onion, quartered

3–4 button mushrooms (optional)

3 litres water

$\frac{1}{2}$ teaspoon salt

2 bay leaves

several parsley stalks, sprigs thyme and black peppercorns

Rinse the chicken carcass, bones and skin, and put them in a saucepan with the other ingredients. Bring to the boil slowly. Skim off any scum that rises to the surface. Simmer the stock for 2–3 hours with the lid partially on (this prevents boiling over but minimizes reduction). Strain and cool quickly. Cover and chill for 24 hours, or freeze. Remove any fat from the surface before using.

Sunkissed Kebabs

I can never cook with yellow peppers in winter... their sunny colour calls for summery days. Thread them on skewers with chunks of firm-textured fish and briny stuffed olives, douse them in honey, lemon and mint, and sizzle them on the barbecue. Sniff the air. Heaven.

How to...

Roast Peppers — *If you have barbecue facilities, peppers can be roasted on the barbecue grill rack and will take on a wonderfully smoky flavour. Alternatively, put the peppers on a rack in an oven preheated to 200°C and cook, turning occasionally with tongs, for about 20 minutes, or until they are blistered and charred. The peppers may also be grilled under a hot grill. Transfer to a board when done and allow to cool. Peel off the skins, slip out the cores and seeds and save any juices for pouring over later.*

Fish Kebabs with Yellow Peppers and Olives

SERVES 6

2 yellow peppers (capsicums) cored, deseeded and cut into smallish chunks

32 fresh bay leaves

245g jar pimiento-stuffed queen olives, drained

3 tablespoons olive oil

750g skinned gurnard fillets, or flathead tails, rinsed and patted dry (or use a firm white fish that will hold together)

1 thin-skinned lemon

1 tablespoon runny honey

2 tablespoons finely chopped mint

$\frac{1}{4}$ teaspoon salt

freshly ground black pepper to taste

Put the yellow peppers, bay leaves and olives in a bowl and mix in 1 tablespoon of oil. Set aside for 15 minutes. Cut the fish into chunks. Peel the lemon, taking the yellow skin only, not the bitter white (easily done with a lemon parer) and cut it into long thin strips. Put it in a bowl with the strained juice of the lemon, the honey, the rest of the oil, the mint, salt, and pepper. Mix well, then add the fish. Thread the fish onto skewers with the yellow pepper chunks, bay leaves and olives.

Cook on a barbecue hot plate over a medium heat, until lightly browned and the fish is just cooked, brushing with some of the juices when necessary. These are superb – straight off the barbecue, or at room temperature.

Salt, Oil and Sea Air Casually arranged bowls of crisp, juicy, salty ingredients, perfumed with herbs, glistening with oil – the perfect food to consume at the water's edge, where the tang of the sea air fills the nostrils and the thundering of the waves resounds in the ears.

Greek Salad

SERVES 6–10

1 small red onion

$\frac{1}{2}$ cup Kalamata olives, drained

1 telegraph cucumber, peeled, halved lengthways, deseeded and cut into chunks

3 ripe tomatoes, cut into wedges

1 green pepper (capsicum), cored, deseeded and cut into strips

1 yellow pepper (capsicum), cored, deseeded and cut into strips

$\frac{1}{2}$ teaspoon salt

1 teaspoon dried Greek rigani or Sicilian oregano (if not available, use fresh marjoram)

freshly ground black pepper to taste

5 tablespoons extra virgin olive oil (preferably Greek oil)

1 tablespoon red wine vinegar

100g feta, in the piece

Slice the red onion into thin rings and transfer to a bowl of ice-cold water. Leave to soak for 1 hour; this makes the onion crisp and removes strong flavours. Drain and pat dry, then put in a large salad bowl with the olives, cucumber, tomatoes and peppers.

Sprinkle the salt and some of the oregano over the salad, then grind on plenty of pepper. Pour over most of the oil, and the vinegar and toss well. Top with the slab of feta, sprinkle the rest of the oregano on top and drizzle with the last tablespoon of oil. Serve immediately, tossing the salad gently at the table.

For Greek Salad with cos lettuce, make the salad as above, omitting the green pepper, using only $\frac{1}{2}$ a cucumber and adding a small cos lettuce. Wash and dry the lettuce, tear into bite-sized pieces and add to the bowl with the tomato and cucumber.

Greek Salad

Hot Peach and Salted Almond Salad

SERVES 4

4 tablespoons light olive oil (choose an oil with a sweet almond flavour rather than an overtly olivey taste)
$\frac{1}{4}$ cup blanched almonds
Maldon sea salt
4 peaches, ripe but firm
$\frac{1}{2}$ teaspoon freshly ground coriander seeds
1 buttercrunch or butterleaf lettuce, washed and dried
1 clove garlic, crushed
2 tablespoons tarragon vinegar, or 1 or 2 tablespoons white wine vinegar with 1 teaspoon chopped tarragon
freshly ground black pepper to taste

Heat 1 tablespoon of the oil in a small frying pan and when it is hot add the almonds. Toss the nuts in the pan until they are lightly browned, then use a slotted spoon to transfer them to a plate lined with absorbent kitchen paper. Sprinkle generously with sea salt. (The nuts can be cooked ahead.)

Peel the peaches, cut into slices and sprinkle with the ground coriander; do this just prior to cooking them or they will discolour.

Break the lettuce leaves into bite-sized pieces and arrange them on a large serving platter. Heat the rest of the oil in a frying pan. Add the garlic and cook until pale golden in colour. Add the peaches, toss gently for 1 minute, then tip in the vinegar. Spoon the peaches and juices over the lettuce, scatter the almonds over and finish with a grind of pepper. Serve immediately.

This salad captures the sweet, juicy delight of summer peaches. Their fruity sweetness is offset with the tang of tarragon vinegar. Combined with a hint of garlic and salted nuts, the effect is stunning. Good on its own as a light starter to a meal, or as an accompanying salad with ham, smoked chicken or quail. For a change, make it with nectarines.

How to...

Use Olive Oil — No other ingredient lends such taste and character to Mediterranean food as olive oil. Nowadays, it's not just Mediterranean people who hold olive oil in such high regard – medical experts around the world are endorsing the inclusion of olive oil in the Western diet. Olive oil is a mono-unsaturated fat, which, among other things, actually lowers cholesterol levels in the body and helps prevent coronary heart disease.

Types of Olive Oil and Uses

Estate bottled olive oil can often be very expensive and is best bought in small quantities for special occasions.

Extra virgin olive oil is 'virgin' oil pressed from sound olives with an acidity level of less than 1%. The solid matter left from the first pressing is used to make regular olive oil, usually marketed as 'pure' olive oil. It will have a higher acidity level and a less strong olivey flavour.

'Light' olive oils are made from further refining.

Use extra virgin olive oil in salads and in dishes where the oil is not heated (or is only warmed) and regular olive oil in cooked dishes.

Unlike wine, olive oil does not improve with age. Buy it in small quantities and use it regularly.

Marinato

SERVES 6–8

1kg skinned and boned fish fillets (choose a firm white
   fish such as gurnard or flathead tails), rinsed and
   patted dry

$\frac{1}{2}$ cup plain flour

150ml olive oil

salt

2 cloves garlic, crushed

500g tomatoes, skinned, cored and diced

2 bay leaves

2 sprigs mint and 2 sprigs oregano, plus extra
   to garnish

100ml dry white wine

3 tablespoons white wine vinegar

$\frac{1}{2}$ cup raisins

freshly ground black pepper to taste

1 teaspoon sugar

$\frac{1}{2}$ teaspoon ground cinnamon

$1\frac{1}{2}$ teaspoons fennel seeds

Coat the fish fillets in flour (do them in 3 batches).
Heat half the oil in a large frying pan over a medium-
high heat. When the oil is very hot, lower in the fillets
and cook them briskly until golden. Turn and cook the
second side. As the pieces of fish are cooked, transfer
them to a shallow dish and sprinkle with salt (add
more oil to the pan if necessary).

Put the remaining 75ml of oil in a clean frying pan
and set over a medium heat. Add the garlic, cook for 1
minute, stirring, then add the tomatoes, herbs, wine
and wine vinegar, raisins, $\frac{1}{4}$ teaspoon of salt, plenty of
black pepper, the sugar, cinnamon and fennel seeds.
Cook for 15 minutes, stirring often, or until fragrant
and pulpy.

Tip the sauce over the fish and leave until cool.
Garnish with mint and oregano and serve at room
temperature.

*This Greek fish dish is good 1–2 days after cooking;
wrap and refrigerate, but bring to room temperature
before serving.*

Cherry Tomato and Black Olive Salad

SERVES 4

2 cups cherry tomatoes

1 cup Kalamata olives, or oil-cured black olives, drained

2 teaspoons capers, drained (for a change, use
   caper berries)

2 tablespoons extra virgin olive oil

1 tablespoon tarragon vinegar, or white wine vinegar

a few pinches of salt

plenty of freshly ground black pepper

1 tablespoon chopped marjoram (or $\frac{1}{4}$ cup tiny basil
   leaves)

If the cherry tomatoes are large, cut them in half. Put
them in a bowl with the olives and capers. In a small
bowl, whisk together the oil, vinegar, salt and pepper,
then pour over the salad. Toss well, adding the
marjoram if using, or scatter the basil leaves over the
top of the salad.

Serve within 2 hours.

Garlicky Gratinated Mussels

SERVES 6–8 AS A FINGER FOOD OR STARTER

36 smallish fresh mussels, cleaned as described below
3 tablespoons soft butter
1 large clove garlic, crushed
grated zest of $\frac{1}{2}$ lemon
$\frac{1}{2}$ teaspoon freshly ground black pepper
1 tablespoon snipped chives
2 rounded tablespoons fresh breadcrumbs
finely chopped parsley to garnish

First clean the mussels. Scrub them under running water with a stiff brush, then pull off the beards. Put the mussels in a large bowl and fill with cold water. Stir the mussels around, then lift out and put in a clean bowl. Repeat the process until the water is clear and grit-free. Leave the mussels to soak for 15 minutes in fresh water. If the water is still gritty, repeat the process until it is clean.

Put the wet mussels in a saucepan with $\frac{1}{4}$ cup of water. Cover the pan and set it over a medium heat. Cook the mussels until they steam open, then use tongs to transfer them to a bowl. Open each mussel, discarding one half of the shell, and check inside for traces of beard etc.

Beat the butter, garlic, lemon zest and black pepper together in a bowl. Mix in the chives and breadcrumbs. Smear a little of the mixture on each mussel, then carefully put the mussels in their half shells in a shallow ovenproof dish.

The mussels can be prepared ahead to this point; keep covered at room temperature for up to 1 hour, or keep refrigerated for several hours before finishing off, but bring to room temperature before grilling.

To finish off, put the mussels under a hot grill for 2–3 minutes or until they are sizzling and golden. Sprinkle with parsley and serve.

Keep the mussels moist with their own juices. After cooking, put the prepared mussels in their half-shells on a tray or plate. If there are no juices pooling in the mussel shells, strain the cooking juices through muslin and anoint the mussels with the juices (don't drown them, just add enough to keep them wet and stop them drying when under the grill).

How to...

Make Breadcrumbs — Soft white crumbs are used in stuffings and fillings to absorb liquids and flavours. They also give body and a light texture, but they do not stay fresh very long as, like bread, they ferment. They will stay fresh in the refrigerator for several days or they can be frozen – it's always useful to have crumbs on hand when time is short (thaw for about 10 minutes at room temperature).

Use a loaf of day-old white bread, remove all crusts and blend the soft crumbs in a food processor or blender until smooth. Store in a plastic bag. Fresh white crumbs may be dried.

Dried white breadcrumbs are used primarily for coating foods which are to be fried.

To make dried breadcrumbs, spread a batch of fresh white breadcrumbs in a baking dish and bake in a low oven preheated to 120°C until dry, but not coloured. Turn them from time to time to ensure they dry evenly. They may take as long as 45 minutes, but don't be tempted to increase the heat. When they are dry, take them out of the oven and blend in a food processor or blender. Pass them through a coarse sieve for a fine result. If they feel at all moist, return them to the baking dish and continue drying in the oven. When completely cool, store them in an airtight container. Dried breadcrumbs will last for many months as the moisture has been driven off and they will not ferment.

Homemade dried breadcrumbs are far superior to commercially made breadcrumbs. The latter often have a musty smell and are usually pulverised and powdery.

Blackened In Ash Vegetables roasted among the hot coals and ashes of a barbecue or open fire, full of smoky flavours, peeled, shredded with the fingers, then splashed with Catalan extra virgin olive oil – this is escalivada in its purest form.

Escalivada

SERVES 6–8

4 long, slim eggplants

2 red peppers (capsicums)

2 yellow peppers (capsicums)

4 small red onions, peeled but roots left on

olive oil

salt

freshly ground black pepper

1 large clove garlic, finely chopped

extra virgin olive oil

Rub the vegetables with oil and put them on a flat baking tray. Cook for about 45 minutes in an oven preheated to 200°C, or until tender and well browned. Transfer the vegetables to a brown paper bag for 10 minutes and leave them to steam. When they are cool enough to handle, peel the vegetables and tear them into shreds with the fingers. Sprinkle the vegetables with salt, grind on some pepper, scatter the garlic over and drizzle with extra virgin olive oil and any pepper juices. Serve hottish or at room temperature.

These days, even in Catalonian restaurants, the vegetables for escalivada are more likely to be cooked in the oven. It's delicious either way. You can serve the vegetables whole or cut into large chunks, as a vegetable dish with salad and bread, or as an accompaniment to grilled or barbecued meat or fish.

The Catalonians like to mash the vegetables to a coarse purée, then to spread the purée on chunks of toasted bread. You can top the escalivada on bread with plump anchovies for added flavour. The dish is then served as tapas.

Tomatoes, garlic bulbs and potatoes can also be cooked this way. Choose firm Roma tomatoes and cook them for 15 minutes only. Use scrubbed small potatoes (or waxy potatoes). I think potatoes are best cooked separately so the skins become crisp, and are not softened by the steam from other vegetables.

In this dish I prefer to use long, slim eggplants, known as Japanese or lady finger eggplants. Onions caramelize as they cook and the sticky residue can easily burn. For that reason it is advisable to first line the tray with baking paper, which can be thrown away after cooking (it beats scrubbing baking trays!).

Baked Summer Vegetables

The kitchen at the back of the beachside taverna, so hot that the flies lie on the floor with their legs in the air in a mock death ritual. The large rectangular pans, blackened and dented from constant use, exuding head-turning aromas. Take a peep. Neat rows of tomatoes, onions, eggplants, and peppers, stuffed to bursting, greet the eye. What to order in a Greek taverna? The decision is made at a glance.

Baked Eggplants with Capers and Tomatoes

SERVES 4

2 large eggplants

salt

2 chopped fresh or canned tomatoes (if fresh, remove the skin)

4 tablespoons olive oil

2 tablespoons capers, drained

2 tablespoons chopped basil, plus extra to garnish

1 clove garlic, crushed

freshly ground black pepper to taste

2 tablespoons dry breadcrumbs

basil leaves to garnish

Cut the eggplants in half lengthways. Score the surface with a sharp knife, sprinkle with salt, then leave to drain in a colander. After 30 minutes, squeeze the juices out of the eggplants, pat the halves dry with absorbent kitchen paper and transfer, cut side up, to a shallow, oiled baking dish (preferably non-stick).

In a small bowl blend the tomato flesh, oil, capers, basil, garlic, and black pepper. Spread over the eggplants, sprinkle the crumbs over the top, then turn them over in the dish so they sit cut side down.

Cook for 30 minutes in an oven preheated to 180°C, then turn them over with a spatula. Cook for a further 15–20 minutes, or until very tender. If the eggplants have not browned, grill them briefly. Cool, then cut into chunks and serve garnished with basil.

This recipe makes a good vegetarian dish, or cut the eggplants into chunks and serve as an antipasto item. It seems to improve in flavour the day after making.

Gratin of Zucchini and Tomato

SERVES 8 OR MORE

5 tablespoons extra virgin olive oil, plus a little extra

600g red onions, thinly sliced

750g smallish firm Roma tomatoes, thinly sliced

750g firm zucchini, trimmed and thinly sliced

1 teaspoon chopped marjoram

2 large cloves garlic, finely chopped

salt

freshly ground black pepper to taste

Put the oil in a large frying pan and set over a low to medium heat. Add the onion and cook, turning often, until soft and just starting to colour. Transfer to 2 medium-sized gratin dishes, level the surface of the onion, then arrange the tomatoes and zucchini on top.

Scatter the marjoram and garlic over, sprinkle each dish with $\frac{1}{4}$ teaspoon salt, grind on some black pepper and drizzle with a little extra oil.

Cook for about 45 minutes in an oven preheated to 200°C, or until browned and bubbling. Serve warmish or at room temperature. If necessary, cool, wrap and refrigerate the dish overnight; bring to room temperature before serving.

Gratin of Zucchini and Tomato

Greek Baked Vegetables

SERVES 8

1 small eggplant
salt
3 carrots (or 3 firm zucchini), peeled, trimmed and cut
    in half lengthways
700g waxy salad potatoes, peeled and cut into
    large chunks
2 yellow peppers (capsicums), cored, deseeded and cut
    into large chunks
4 firm medium tomatoes, halved (preferably Roma
    tomatoes)
2 medium red onions, peeled and cut into quarters
    through the base
12 large cloves garlic, peeled
$\frac{1}{2}$ cup olive oil
1 teaspoon dried Greek rigani or Sicilian oregano (if not
    available, use fresh marjoram)
freshly ground black pepper to taste

Slice the eggplant into large cubes, put in a colander
and sprinkle with salt. Leave for 20 minutes, then pat
dry with absorbent kitchen paper.

Put the prepared vegetables in a large roasting tin,
with the onions and garlic on top, and pour in $\frac{3}{4}$ cup of
water. Pour over the oil, sprinkle with oregano and $\frac{1}{2}$
teaspoon of salt, and grind on some pepper. Cover with
aluminium foil.

Bake the vegetables for 45 minutes in an oven
preheated to 180°C. Increase the heat to 225°C,
remove the foil and cook for 30–45 minutes more,
turning the vegetables occasionally, or until they are
tender and lightly charred. Serve hottish or at room
temperature.

*Most Greek cookbooks contain a recipe for baked
summer vegetables, but the vegetables are often
swimming in oil, or they turn sloppy and don't become
crisp. The trick is to provide just enough liquid and oil
so that the vegetables can steam and become tender
during the initial cooking period, and turn crisp and
golden when the cover is removed. When you get it
right, they're delicious.*

Ratatouille

SERVES 6–8

2 medium eggplants, cut into large cubes
salt
2 medium onions, finely sliced
2 cloves garlic, crushed
a handful of basil leaves
150ml olive oil
3 large peppers (capsicums), red, yellow, and green,
    cored, deseeded and cut into thick chunks
500g ripe tomatoes, skinned and diced
500g small zucchini, sliced into thick chunks
freshly ground black pepper to taste

Put the eggplant cubes in a colander and sprinkle with
salt; leave to drain for 30 minutes. Put the onions,
garlic and basil into a large saucepan with 75ml of the
oil. Cook on a very low heat, stirring often, for about
20 minutes, or until tender. Add the peppers, cover the
pan with a lid and cook gently for 10 minutes, then
add the tomatoes, cover with the lid again and cook
for 20 minutes.

Pat the eggplant cubes dry with absorbent kitchen
paper. Heat the rest of the oil in a frying pan over a
medium heat and when hot, add the eggplant cubes.
Cook, tossing often, until lightly browned and tender.

Add to the tomato mixture, along with the
zucchini, $\frac{3}{4}$ teaspoon of salt and a good grinding of
black pepper. Mix everything together, bring to a
gentle boil then turn the heat to low. Partially cover
with a lid and cook gently for about 30 minutes or
until tender; if the ratatouille is very liquid, cook
without a lid.

Serve hot or at room temperature.

*No matter how you make ratatouille, olive oil and
tomatoes are the 2 integral ingredients. It usually
contains peppers, either single colour or a variety, and
may also contain eggplant, zucchini and/or potatoes
and may be flavoured with garlic, coriander seeds, basil
or parsley.*

*My favourite way to have ratatouille is highly
perfumed with basil, achieved by first stewing the onion
and basil leaves in olive oil. The gentle heat coaxes
every scrap of flavour from the basil yet, once mixed
with the other ingredients, the clove-like aroma and*

taste of the basil melds all the flavours together, rather than dominating the dish. Some people prefer the vegetables softish and very tender, while others like them crunchy. I enjoy it best when the ingredients are cooked longer – as with any stew, you get more flavour that way. Ratatouille keeps well for 1–2 days and can be served at room temperature or reheated.

Tomatoes Stuffed with Couscous

SERVES 6

6 large, ripe red outdoor tomatoes

salt

extra virgin olive oil

125g couscous

2 cloves garlic, crushed

1 tablespoon chopped parsley

1 teaspoon chopped marjoram (or a few pinches dried marjoram)

2 teaspoons lemon juice

$\frac{1}{2}$ cup pine nuts, toasted

freshly ground black pepper to taste

$\frac{1}{2}$ cup black olives, stoned and chopped

Dressing

2 tablespoons sieved tomato pulp

2 tablespoons extra virgin olive oil

1 teaspoon lemon juice

few pinches salt

freshly ground black pepper to taste

Slice a cap off the flower end of the tomatoes (the opposite end to the stalk end). Scoop out the seeds and pulp and drain in a sieve. Turn the tomatoes upside down on a board and leave to drain.

Put 125ml of water in a small saucepan with $\frac{1}{2}$ teaspoon of salt and 1 teaspoon of oil. Bring to the boil, then tip in the couscous. Stir, then cover with a lid and leave for 15 minutes. Fluff up with a fork, then transfer to a bowl.

Add 1 tablespoon of oil, the garlic, parsley, marjoram, lemon juice, pine nuts, black pepper and a few pinches of salt. Mix in the olives (if they are salty, you may not need any salt).

Pile the mixture into the drained tomatoes, mounding the top, and arrange them on a plate. Push some of the tomato pulp through a sieve. Put 2 tablespoons of the pulp in a small bowl and add the rest of the dressing ingredients. Blend together and spoon over the tomatoes. Serve with pita bread and a spinach salad.

It is essential to use ripe red tomatoes for this dish. If they're not available, leave the recipe until they are. The filling is very tasty and it can be used in other ways, but cut back on the quantity of salt.

Stuffed Vegetables with Red Onion and Tomato Filling

SERVES 8

Filling

4 medium red onions, finely sliced

3 tablespoons olive oil

2 large cloves garlic, crushed

2 tablespoons chopped parsley

$\frac{1}{2}$ teaspoon salt

freshly ground black pepper to taste

4 tomatoes, skinned, deseeded and cut into slivers

Crumb Mixture

$\frac{1}{2}$ cup soft white breadcrumbs

$\frac{1}{4}$ teaspoon salt

freshly ground black pepper to taste

1 tablespoon chopped fresh marjoram (or 1 teaspoon dried marjoram)

1 tablespoon chopped parsley

2 tablespoons freshly grated Italian parmesan cheese

1 tablespoon olive oil

Vegetables

a selection of the following:

scallopini (yellow or green button squash), large Roma tomatoes, zucchini, red and yellow peppers (capsicums), slim eggplants (Japanese eggplants)

Seasonings

olive oil

salt

freshly ground black pepper

pesto (optional)

anchovies in oil (optional)

freshly grated Italian parmesan cheese

chopped parsley

Prepare the red onion filling first, and then make the crumb mixture.

Put the onions in a large frying pan with the olive oil. Cook over a low heat for about 10 minutes until soft (don't allow the onions to colour). Add the garlic and cook for 3–4 minutes more, then stir in the parsley, salt, pepper and tomatoes.

In a bowl mix the breadcrumbs, salt, pepper, marjoram, parsley, parmesan and olive oil.

Next prepare all the vegetables, reserving the scooped out flesh. Trim the scallopini so they will sit flat, then slice off a cap. Use a teaspoon to scoop out the filling. Lie the tomatoes on their sides and slice off a cap. Scoop out the flesh to make a cavity. Cut a lengthways strip of skin off the zucchini and scoop out some flesh. Cut the peppers in half and cut out the seeds, but leave the cores on to hold them together.

The eggplants can be prepared in 2 different ways. Either cut them in half lengthways and scoop out some flesh to make a cavity before cooking, or cook them whole, scoop out the flesh, stuff and cook. If cooking whole, the eggplants need to be blanched in boiling water first. Drop them into a pan of boiling salted water (2 at a time) and cook for 1 minute. When cool enough to handle, lie them on their sides, slice off a cap and scoop out the flesh.

Arrange the prepared vegetables in oiled roasting pans, grouping the fat vegetables together in one pan and the flat ones together in a separate pan. Sprinkle the cavities with salt and pepper.

Transfer half the tomato and onion filling to the crumb mixture and mix well. Pile the rest of the tomato and onion mixture into some of the vegetables (if liked, spread a little pesto into the cavities first, or add an anchovy).

Finely chop the scooped-out vegetable flesh and add it to the other half of the tomato mixture. Pile it into the rest of the vegetables. Drizzle the vegetables with olive oil and sprinkle with parmesan cheese. Bake them in an oven preheated to 225°C, for 15–20 minutes or until browned and appetising to the eye. Serve hottish or at room temperature sprinkled with parsley.

Stuffed vegetables are enjoyed in all the Mediterranean countries. Stuffings are made from meat, chicken, rice, pulses and vegetables and many have heavy garlic, herb or spice accents. The vegetables are usually generously drizzled with olive oil, making them rich and delicious, and cooked until they are fork-tender.

A Catalan Treasure Small, dark-red and smoky, the nyora pepper yields its magic to Romesco, a grunty sauce flavoured with garlic, thickened with toasted ground nuts and fried bread and sharpened with good red wine vinegar.

Tuna Steaks with Romesco Sauce

SERVES 4

Romesco Sauce

2 large tomatoes

2 small, hot red chillies

2 large red peppers (capsicums)

25g blanched almonds

25g hazelnuts

50ml extra virgin olive oil (choose a mild Spanish oil)

1 slice day-old white toast bread

2 large cloves garlic, crushed

$\frac{1}{4}$ teaspoon salt

1 $\frac{1}{2}$ teaspoons red wine vinegar

Tuna

1 tablespoon olive oil

1 tablespoon clarified butter

4 small tuna steaks, cut 2–3cm thick

flour

salt

freshly ground black pepper

Put the tomatoes and chillies on an oven tray and grill under a high heat. Remove the chillies when they are charred, but grill the tomatoes on both sides until their skins split and blacken. Roughly chop the chillies, discarding seeds if preferred. Skin the tomatoes and chop the flesh, discarding seeds and cores. Grill the peppers until charred, cool, remove skin, cores and seeds and chop the flesh.

Toast the nuts in a hot oven until lightly golden; about 7 minutes for the almonds and 10 minutes for the hazelnuts. Put the hazelnuts in an old cloth, form it into a bundle and rub off the skins.

Heat 1$\frac{1}{2}$ tablespoons of the oil in a small frying pan over a medium heat. Fry the bread until golden, then wipe out the pan and add the rest of the oil and the garlic. Cook gently until it is a pale golden colour. Put the nuts and fried bread (broken into pieces) into a food processor and tip in the garlic and all the oil. Process to a paste, then add the peppers, chillies, tomatoes, salt and vinegar and process again until well blended. Turn into a bowl and serve; if not for immediate use, cover and chill (use within 24 hours).

Heat a large heavy-based frying pan over a medium-high heat. When it is hot, add the oil, allow the oil to get hot, then add the butter. Meanwhile, dust the tuna steaks with flour. Cook for 1$\frac{1}{2}$–2 minutes each side, depending on how rare you prefer the tuna. Transfer tuna to a heated serving dish, sprinkle with salt and pepper and serve immediately with the Romesco Sauce.

Romesco is a Catalan sauce (or sometimes a Catalan fish stew flavoured with Romesco sauce) based on the nyora pepper, a small, dark-red pepper, usually dried, which has a bite to it – sort of like a cross between a sweet red pepper and a mild-intensity chilli. It has many uses. The sauce can be thinned with more oil, which turns it into a pouring sauce. In this thickened form, its grunty texture, smoky resonance and finishing jab of acid make a great counterpoint to the deceptively light tuna steaks. It makes a good plate mate for roasted, grilled or barbecued chicken and pork and for seafood.

Don't overcook the tuna; it is wonderfully light and tender to eat when cooked rare or medium rare.

Chargrilled vegetables for Romesco Sauce

Terrific Tomato Tarts

'Ladybirds on green grass', my young friend Alice murmured to herself as she watched me nestle halved cherry tomatoes together on rounds of puff pastry smeared generously with pesto. For a 'red' theme, swap the pesto for fresh tomato 'jam'. Either way, these tarts are extraordinarily good and extraordinarily easy to assemble.

Tomato Tarts

MAKES 10 – ALLOW 1 PER PERSON AS A STARTER, 2–3 AS A MAIN COURSE

Tomato Jam

4 Roma tomatoes, skinned

2 tablespoons extra virgin olive oil

1 large clove garlic, crushed

1 tablespoon tomato paste

salt

freshly ground black pepper to taste

Tarts

5 sheets purchased ready rolled puff pastry, thawed

60–70 cherry tomatoes (maybe more)

1 egg beaten with a pinch of salt

Pesto

2 cups fresh basil leaves, tightly packed

salt

2 large cloves garlic, crushed

3 tablespoons pine nuts

50 ml extra virgin olive oil

4 tablespoons freshly grated Italian parmesan cheese

2 tablespoons freshly grated romano cheese (if not available, use 6 tablespoons parmesan cheese)

Cut the tomatoes into quarters and flick out the seeds. Cut out the cores, then dice the flesh. Put the oil and garlic in a small saucepan, set over a medium heat and cook for 1–2 minutes until softened, then add the tomatoes and tomato paste. Season with a pinch of salt and a little black pepper and stir well. Cook gently for about 15–20 minutes, or until thick and pulpy; stir often. Transfer to a small dish. (The tomato jam should be very thick; it can be made the day before.)

Cut out 10 rounds of pastry 13cm in diameter. Put the pastry rounds on a lined baking tray (prepare 3–4 at a time, keeping the remaining pastry rounds covered). Put a dollop of pesto or tomato jam in the centre of each and spread it to within 1cm of the edges. Halve the cherry tomatoes and arrange them skin side facing up, on each round of pastry.

Pesto is quickly made in a food processor. Put the basil leaves, a pinch of salt, the garlic, pine nuts and oil in the bowl of a processor fitted with the chopping blade. Process until blended. Transfer to a bowl and mix in the cheeses by hand. If the pesto is too thick, thin it with a little more oil, or a little warm water. Cover the surface with plastic wrap and set aside until required.

Brush the exposed pastry rims with beaten egg. Bake the tarts for 10 minutes in a hot oven preheated to 225°C, or until the pastry is a rich golden brown. Serve warm.

the end golden weather

When summer is peaking and passing, enjoy the outdoors before the cold puts an end to leisurely lunches in sheltered spots. Food can be a little richer, a little more substantial...

of the

SPICY AND COOLING
Rib-eye Roast with Moroccan Flavours
Cucumber Salad
Stewed Peppers

MELTING FETA WITH PRAWNS
Greek Prawns Baked with Feta

THE FAINTING PRIEST
Imam Bayildi

SPANISH TUNA FOR LUNCH
Spanish Tuna with Green Pepper and Pine Nuts

PRAWNS IN PICADA
Prawns with Picada Sauce

A NIÇOISE PIE
Pissaladière

REVISITING AÏOLI
Smoked Fish Platter with Aïoli

DRIZZLE WITH CHERMOULA
Hot-smoked Salmon with Chermoula Dressing and Sautéed Limes

Spicy and Cooling Drizzle roasted beef with a darkly rich mysterious sauce, fragrant with cinnamon, cumin, ginger and coriander, with a kick like a mule. Temper the fiery mix with chunks of cooling cucumber and sweet pepper, refreshed with a squeeze of lemon...

Rib-eye Roast with Moroccan Flavours

SERVES ABOUT 8

1.5kg boneless rib-eye beef (scotch fillet)

2 tablespoons olive oil

salt

Marinade

100ml olive oil

juice of 2 lemons

2 tablespoons dry white wine or sherry

1 small onion, very finely chopped

$\frac{1}{2}$ cup canned Italian tomatoes, mashed

8 pitted prunes, chopped

4 tablespoons chopped coriander

1 tablespoon finely grated ginger

2 teaspoons toasted ground cumin (see page 27)

2 teaspoons chilli powder

1 teaspoon ground cinnamon

$\frac{1}{2}$ teaspoon freshly ground black pepper

1 teaspoon salt

Trim excess fat from the beef, remove any silvery skin, then tie it in shape with string. Mix all the marinade ingredients together in a large, shallow dish and add the beef. Turn the meat in the marinade, cover, and refrigerate for 3–4 hours, turning the meat in the marinade occasionally.

Remove the beef from the refrigerator 1 hour before cooking. Scrape off the marinade with a flat-bladed knife and pat the joint very dry with absorbent kitchen paper. Heat the oil in a roasting pan (choose one in which the meat fits snugly) and when it is hot put in the beef. Brown quickly on both sides, then transfer it to an oven preheated to 200°C. Roast for 30–40 minutes, turning once and basting twice (30 minutes for rare, 40 minutes for medium-rare). Remove the beef from the oven and sprinkle 1 teaspoon of salt all over the beef. Let the meat rest for 15 minutes, loosely covered with aluminium foil, before slicing.

Meanwhile, put the marinade in a saucepan and cook gently for 10 minutes until softened and pulpy. Tuck absorbent kitchen paper around the edges of the chopping board to absorb juices and place the meat on the board. Slice the meat into pieces about 5mm thick. Rest the sliced meat for a minute, mop up the juices, then transfer to a heated serving platter. Serve immediately with the sauce.

Buttered couscous and a mélange of seasonal vegetables make good hot accompaniments. The roasted beef is equally delicious cold (but slice it more thinly), served with either Cucumber Salad or Stewed Peppers.

Cucumber Salad

SERVES 6

1 small red onion, peeled, halved and finely sliced

1 large telegraph cucumber (or 2 small Lebanese
cucumbers)

1 small yellow pepper (capsicum), cored, deseeded and
cut into thin strips

1 small red pepper (capsicum), cored, deseeded
and diced

2 tablespoons chopped flat leaf parsley

1 large clove garlic, crushed

1 small red chilli, deseeded and finely chopped
(optional)

4 tablespoons extra virgin olive oil

1 $\frac{1}{2}$ tablespoons lemon juice

$\frac{3}{4}$ teaspoon salt

freshly ground black pepper to taste

2 ripe tomatoes, chilled

Soak the onion in cold water for 15 minutes, drain and
dry with absorbent kitchen paper. Peel the cucumber,
trim the ends, then slice into 4 pieces lengthways. Cut
away the seeds then chop the flesh (if using Lebanese
cucumbers, there is no need to peel or seed them). Put
the onion and cucumber in a bowl with the peppers,
parsley, garlic, chilli (if using), oil, lemon juice, salt and
pepper. Toss well, then cover and chill for 2 hours.

Just before serving, quarter the chilled tomatoes,
remove the cores and flick out the seeds. Chop the flesh
and add to the salad. Toss well and serve immediately.

*This salad is good served with smoked fish or
barbecued chicken or, if the chilli is left out, it makes a
cooling accompaniment to the Rib-eye Roast with
Moroccan Flavours.*

Stewed Peppers

SERVES 6–8

3 large red peppers (capsicums)

3 large yellow peppers (capsicums)

$\frac{1}{4}$ cup extra virgin olive oil

2 cloves garlic

$\frac{1}{4}$ teaspoon salt

freshly ground black pepper to taste

1 tablespoon balsamic vinegar

1 tablespoon chopped parsley

Cut the peppers in half, remove cores and seeds, then
cut each half into 4 pieces. Dry with kitchen paper.
Heat the oil in a large frying pan set over a medium
heat and when hot, add the peppers. Fry for a few
minutes, tossing often, then cover with a lid and cook
on a medium heat for 15–20 minutes, or until tender,
stirring occasionally.

Remove lid, add the garlic and increase the heat.
Cook for a few minutes more to evaporate excess
juices (what remains should be syrupy). Sprinkle with
salt, grind on some pepper and add the balsamic
vinegar. Toss well, transfer to a serving bowl and leave
to cool. Sprinkle on parsley before serving.

The peppers can be cooked a day ahead; cover and
refrigerate, but bring to room temperature before
serving. Serve as a side dish with the Hot-smoked
Salmon (see page 96), Rib-eye Roast (see opposite
page) or with Italian dishes.

Melting Feta with Prawns Tender plump prawns, swathed in a flavoursome sauce, dotted with melting cubes of feta cheese. Awesome!

Greek Prawns Baked with Feta

SERVES 6–10

1kg green king prawns

$\frac{1}{2}$ cup olive oil

1 medium onion, finely chopped

2 cloves garlic, crushed

2 x 400g cans Italian tomatoes, very well mashed

$\frac{1}{4}$ teaspoon salt

freshly ground black pepper to taste

2 tablespoons coarsely chopped parsley

100g feta cheese

Prepare the prawns. If frozen, thaw slowly in the refrigerator. Twist off their heads, peel off three-quarters of their shells, leaving the small piece of the tail intact. Slit down the back of each prawn with a sharp knife and extract the black or orangey red vein running right down the length. Rinse the prawns and pat dry with absorbent kitchen paper.

Pour the oil into a large saucepan, add the onion, then cover and cook gently until tender. Remove the lid, add the garlic and cook for 5–10 minutes more, or until lightly golden. Add the tomatoes, bring to the boil, then turn to low and simmer gently for 30 minutes. Add salt, pepper and parsley. The sauce may be prepared several hours ahead to this point. When ready to cook the prawns, reheat the sauce and add the prepared prawns. Stir gently, then transfer the mixture to a shallow ovenproof dish. Crumble the feta over and bake for about 12 minutes in an oven preheated to 170°C, or until the feta is lightly coloured and the prawns are cooked through. Serve hot.

How to...

Use Feta — Feta is a fresh cheese usually made from sheep's milk, but sometimes from goat's milk, or a mix of the two milks, or sometimes from cow's milk. Salt is used to preserve feta and the resulting cheese can be very salty. To draw out the excess salt, follow the Greek practice of soaking the feta in water for 10–30 minutes before using it (this is not recommended for creamy types of feta – just the more solid crumbly ones). Pat the feta dry with absorbent kitchen paper before carrying on with the recipe.

Although feta is used predominantly in salads, it can also be cooked. Crumble the feta into small cubes, or cut it into thin slices. Put the feta on a baking tray lined with baking paper or aluminium foil and cook under a hot grill until brown. The feta doesn't melt or spread. It colours quickly and tastes very nutty, and has a slightly chewy consistency.

Add it to salads and open sandwiches, or serve it on top of vegetable dishes, or in flans and pies. Slabs of feta can be dusted with flour, brushed with egg, coated in fine breadcrumbs and fried in bubbling oil until golden. Serve with a salad of baby leaves.

The Fainting Priest The story goes that the priest swooned when he was served these eggplants. Don't ask a Greek to explain why if a Turk is within earshot, and vice versa. Trust me, it must have been the amount of garlic used.

Imam Bayildi

SERVES 4

4 medium eggplants

salt

$\frac{1}{2}$ cup olive oil

2 large onions, thinly sliced

2 large cloves garlic, crushed

400g can Italian tomatoes, mashed

2 tablespoons coarsely chopped parsley

freshly ground black pepper to taste

$\frac{1}{2}$ teaspoon sugar

juice of 1 lemon

Trim the eggplants then peel off strips of the skin lengthways, leaving alternate strips of skin and exposed flesh. Sprinkle well with salt and leave to drain for 1 hour in a colander.

Heat $\frac{1}{4}$ cup of the oil in a large frying pan over a low heat. Add the onions, cover the pan and cook gently for 10 minutes, or until soft. Add the garlic and cook for a further 2 minutes, then add the tomatoes, parsley, black pepper and $\frac{1}{2}$ teaspoon of salt. Cook, uncovered, for 10 minutes, then set aside. Heat the remaining oil in a deep, heavy-based saucepan or casserole over a medium-high heat (this helps confine the splattering, but a frying pan can be used). Pat the eggplants dry with absorbent kitchen paper, then lower them carefully into the hot oil. Fry quickly, turning with tongs, until they are evenly browned. Transfer to a plate to cool briefly.

Cut a slit in each eggplant, taking care not to cut right the way through, and force it open to form a cavity. Spoon some of the stuffing inside each cavity, then put the eggplants in a shallow ovenproof dish (choose one in which they fit snugly). Spoon the rest of the tomato mixture on top. Mix the sugar and lemon juice with $\frac{1}{2}$ cup water and pour this around the eggplants. Cover the dish with a lid or a double thickness of aluminium foil and bake for 45–60 minutes, or until tender, in an oven preheated to 180°C. Remove the lid or foil and bake for 10–15 minutes more, until the juices are reduced and syrupy. Transfer to a dish, pour the juices over, then allow the eggplant to cool to room temperature before serving.

The origin of this mouth-watering dish is highly controversial: the Greeks claim it as theirs, but the Turks, who can lay claim to the word Imam, state just as fiercely that the dish originated in Turkey. The story behind the name, told by both, goes something like this: A priest (an Imam) nearly fainted (or did faint – depends on the story-teller) when he was served this dish, hence the name, fainting priest. Whether he fainted because the dish smelled and looked so good, or because of how much garlic or olive oil was used in the making of it, is just another point to make Greek and Turkish blood boil.

Whatever, it makes a superb vegetarian main course, but it is also good when cut into morsels and served as mezes. Like me, it's always better after a little siesta, so make it the day before serving; store it covered and refrigerated, but bring the dish to room temperature before serving.

Spanish Tuna for Lunch Large flakes of canned Spanish tuna, submerged in an oily tomato sauce flecked with pine nuts, made for bread-dipping and Indian summer lunching.

Spanish Tuna with Green Pepper and Pine Nuts

SERVES 10

½ cup olive oil

50g pine nuts

4 large green peppers (capsicums), cored, deseeded and
   cut into large chunks

1.5kg ripe tomatoes, peeled and chopped (preferably
   outdoor tomatoes)

½ teaspoon salt

freshly ground black pepper to taste

200g can Spanish tuna in oil, drained (don't flake it – it
   looks better on top of the cooked dish in large pieces)

grated zest of 1 lemon

Put ¼ cup of the olive oil in a large frying pan over a low to medium heat. When the oil is hot, add the pine nuts. Cook gently until lightly coloured, moving the pine nuts around with a slotted spoon, then using the spoon transfer them to a side plate.

Add the rest of the olive oil to the pan and increase the heat to medium. Drop in the peppers and cook for 7–10 minutes, tossing often, or until starting to brown. Tip in the tomatoes and bring to the boil. Lower the heat a little and cook gently, uncovered, for about an hour, or until the tomato mixture is well reduced and pulpy; stir often, especially towards the end of cooking. Stir the salt through and grind on some pepper. Transfer to a bowl and leave to cool (overnight is fine; cover and refrigerate).

When cool, stir through the pine nuts, then add the tuna. Stir gently once or twice, just to break up the tuna a little, then sprinkle the lemon zest over the top and grind on some more pepper.

If the tomatoes are not naturally sweet, add a teaspoon of sugar when you start cooking them. The dish keeps well, covered and refrigerated, for 1–2 days.

Spanish Tuna with Green Pepper and Pine Nuts

Prawns in Picada This eclipses every prawn dish I've ever made. It's a rich, succulent, sensuous treat that will send prawn-lovers into a feeding frenzy.

Prawns with Picada Sauce

SERVES 6–10

1kg green king prawns

$\frac{1}{2}$ cup olive oil

1 slice stale white bread (dry the bread at room
    temperature)

$\frac{3}{4}$ cup pine nuts

6 large cloves garlic, peeled

2 tablespoons chopped parsley, plus extra to garnish

salt

1 $\frac{1}{2}$ cups fish stock or light stock

$\frac{3}{4}$ teaspoon sweet paprika

4 fresh bay leaves

Prepare the prawns first. If frozen, thaw slowly in the refrigerator. Twist off their heads, then peel off their shells, leaving the small piece on the tail intact. Slit down the back of each prawn with a sharp knife and gently extract the black or orangey red vein running right down the length. Rinse the prawns and pat dry with absorbent kitchen paper.

Heat a little of the oil in a small frying pan over a medium-high heat. Add the slice of bread and fry quickly on each side until brown. Leave the bread to cool, then slice off the crusts.

Put the pine nuts in a shallow ovenproof dish and toast them for 5–8 minutes, or until golden, in an oven preheated to 180°C (keep an eye on them; they colour quickly). Crush 3 cloves of garlic and put them in a food processor along with the pine nuts, chopped parsley, roughly chopped bread and a few pinches of salt. Add 2–3 tablespoons of the stock, then process until finely chopped. (Don't over-process the mixture; it should have texture. If you don't have a food processor, you can crush the ingredients in a mortar with a pestle.)

Heat the rest of the oil in a large frying pan over a medium heat and add the remaining 3 cloves of garlic.

Cook until the garlic turns brown, then remove it and discard. Remove the pan from the heat and leave to cool for a few minutes. Stir in the paprika and bay leaves, cook for 1 minute, then pour in the rest of the stock and add $\frac{1}{4}$ teaspoon of salt. Bring to a gentle boil and cook for 10 minutes, or until reduced by half, then add the prawns. Cook until the undersides are pink (2–3 minutes) then turn and cook the other sides until pink and just cooked through. Stir the pine nut mixture into the pan and turn and coat the prawns with the picada. Turn into a hot serving dish and serve immediately, garnished with parsley.

Catalan in origin, picada is best described as a sauce base, made from ground or pounded nuts (almonds, pine nuts, hazelnuts), fried bread, olive oil and garlic, to which seasonings are added. This is traditionally made in a mortar with a pestle, and the ingredients are pounded to a paste. A food processor doesn't achieve this – if you want a very smooth picada, pound the nuts in a mortar first, then finish it off in a food processor.

Fish Stock

1 fish frame, rinsed

peeled rind of 1 small lemon

1 onion, sliced

1 carrot, sliced

1 bay leaf

blade of mace

a few peppercorns

2.25 litres cold water

Put all the ingredients in a saucepan. Bring to the boil, then lower the heat and simmer for 20 minutes. Strain immediately. Refrigerate when cool. Use within 24 hours or freeze for up to 4 weeks.

A Niçoise Pie A pillow-soft crust housing a perky little filling of sweet onions, thyme and garlic, crisscrossed with anchovies and Niçoise olives...

Pissaladière

SERVES AT LEAST 8

Crust

½ cup milk

1 level tablespoon dried yeast

225g (about 1 ¾ cups) plain flour

½ teaspoon salt

50g butter

Filling

2 tablespoons olive oil

2 tablespoons butter

1.5kg large mild onions, finely sliced (chilling the onions first can help minimize tears during peeling and chopping)

1 tablespoon finely chopped thyme

2 cloves garlic, crushed

freshly ground black pepper to taste

freshly grated nutmeg to taste

few pinches salt

3–4 small cans anchovy fillets in oil, drained and fillets split lengthways (I find the cheaper anchovy fillets are too squishy; try the ones rolled around capers, they seem a little more robust)

small black Niçoise olives and extra olive oil to garnish

Put the milk in a saucepan and heat until just warm. Sprinkle the yeast granules over it, then set aside until the yeast dissolves, stirring occasionally. Reserve 25g (about 3 tablespoons) flour and sift the remaining 200g of the flour into a bowl with the salt, then rub in the butter with your fingertips. When the yeast has dissolved, add the milk mixture and blend together with a wooden spoon until a ball forms.

Use the remaining flour to dust the work surface and to stop the dough from sticking during kneading. Knead for 7–10 minutes, until the dough is elastic and springy, then place in a warmed, buttered bowl. Turn the dough over to coat it on all sides with butter, then cover with a damp cloth. Leave in a warm place until doubled in bulk (about 2 hours).

To make the filling, put the oil and butter in a large, wide saucepan. Add the onions and cook gently for about 40 minutes, stirring often, or until very tender and lightly browned (stir often towards the end of cooking). Add the thyme and garlic and cook for 5 minutes more. Grind on plenty of black pepper, grate some nutmeg over and add the salt. Stir to combine, then leave to cool for 10 minutes (if the mixture is very moist, drain it briefly in a sieve).

To assemble, turn the dough onto a work surface and roll into a round. Line into a 32cm pizza tray (alternatively, cook it on a terracotta pizza stone, according to the manufacturer's instructions). Build the sides of the dough up a little around the edges to prevent the filling from oozing out.

Spread the filling over the dough, then make a lattice pattern with the anchovies. Stud with olives, then leave the pie to rest (prove) in a warm spot for 30 minutes. Brush the tops of the olives with a little olive oil if they look dry, then bake the Pissaladière for about 30 minutes in an oven preheated to 220°C. If the top colours, but the base is still not ready, loosely drape a piece of aluminium foil over the top of the pie. Remove from the oven and cool for 10 minutes before cutting into slices (easily done with scissors).

The addition of milk to the yeast crust of this version of the famous Niçoise pizza gives a tender crust. If you want to take a shortcut, substitute a ready-made pizza base for the soft dough crust.

Revisiting Aïoli Before the sunny days fade into a memory, lay a cloth on the lawn, bring forth a mountainous platter laden with smoked fish, potatoes and aïoli. Chink the glasses as you overflow them with bubbly and drink to the simple pleasures of life.

Smoked Fish Platter with Aïoli

SERVES 6

Aïoli

2 cloves garlic

salt

dab of Dijon-style mustard

3 egg yolks, at room temperature

300ml olive oil

1–2 tablespoons lemon juice

1 smoked fish of your choice

700g waxy salad potatoes, scrubbed

6 quail's eggs (or 3–4 hen's eggs)

3 tablespoons chopped herbs (parsley, chives, chervil)

12 tiny gherkins, drained and sliced

Crush the garlic on a board with a few pinches of salt; it should turn into a paste. Make mayonnaise (see instructions on page 24), blending the crushed garlic with the egg yolks and seasonings; be generous with the lemon and salt. If the mayonnaise is very thick, thin it with fresh boiled (cooled) water.

Take the fish off the bones, discarding skin, scales and bones.

Steam the potatoes until tender, then peel when cool and cut into quarters or slices.

Cook the quail's eggs for 5 minutes in gently boiling water, or cook hen's eggs for 7 minutes. Cool under running water and peel carefully, then cut in half.

Mound the smoked fish into the centre of a platter and arrange the potatoes around the edge of the dish. Spoon the aïoli over. Arrange chopped herbs, quail's eggs and gherkins on top and serve with warm, crusty bread.

In spring, add 400g asparagus to the dish, or a clutch of slim green beans, lightly blanched and chopped.

How to...

Boil Eggs — The description 'hard-boiled eggs' is a misnomer. Eggs are more palatable and more easily digested if lightly cooked. When you first lower the eggs into the water, carefully roll them around the pot for a few seconds. This sets the yolk in the centre of the egg.

To prevent the shells from cracking during cooking, use the point of a dressmaking pin to prick the rounded end of each egg, where there is a small air sac. The pinhole acts like an escape valve: as the contents of the egg swell during cooking, they force the air out of the air sac, preventing the shell from cracking.

Having the eggs at room temperature and bringing them slowly to the boil also helps.

Be careful where you store eggs. Eggshells are porous and can absorb strong odours. If possible, store eggs in an egg carton, in the closed drawer of the refrigerator, away from strong-smelling foods.

To make eggs last longer, store them with the pointed end facing down (they usually come this way in the carton). This prevents the air sac from breaking, which helps maintain the quality of the egg.

The difference between...

Fish can either be 'cold-smoked' (for example, salmon, which is cured, but not cooked by faintly warm smoke), or 'hot-smoked' – like most commercially smoked fish.

When correctly carried out, hot-smoking involves preliminary cold-smoking at around 1–30°C, then the temperature is raised and the food briefly hot-smoked. The low smoking temperature ensures that the smoke has time to fully permeate the fish, and so flavour it, and that sufficient moisture loss occurs, extending the keeping time of the fish. The final blast of heat forms a skin and improves the colour, as well as enhancing the surface flavour.

Drizzle with Chermoula Take a platter of succulent flakes of hot-smoked salmon dripping oil, giant shell-pink prawns, pea-green chunks of avocado smartened with lime, and Chermoula, Morocco's wickedly sexy sauce...

Hot-smoked Salmon with Chermoula Dressing and Sautéed Limes

SERVES 6 AS A MAIN COURSE, OR MORE AS A LIGHT DISH

Chermoula Dressing

$\frac{1}{2}$ cup (well packed) chopped coriander

$\frac{1}{2}$ cup (well packed) chopped flat leaf parsley

3 cloves garlic, roughly chopped

3 tablespoons lemon juice

2 teaspoons ground cumin

$\frac{1}{2}$ teaspoon paprika

$\frac{1}{2}$ teaspoon chilli powder (optional)

$\frac{1}{4}$ teaspoon ground cinnamon

$\frac{1}{2}$ teaspoon salt

$\frac{1}{2}$ cup extra virgin olive oil

1 cup fine burghul

salt

750g hot-smoked salmon

16–20 green king prawns (if frozen, thaw them slowly in the refrigerator)

3 tablespoons extra virgin olive oil

1 tablespoon lime juice

2 hot red chillies, finely chopped (discard seeds if preferred)

3 fresh limes

olive oil

2 ripe but firm avocados

Make the Chermoula Dressing first. Put all the dressing ingredients except the oil in a food processor and blend until smooth. With the machine running, pour in the oil. Transfer to a bowl, taste and adjust seasoning if necessary, then cover and refrigerate until required.

Put the burghul in a sieve and rinse it to wash off any dust. Transfer it to a bowl and pour on very hot water to cover; soak for 30 minutes. Drain, then squeeze out as much moisture as possible. Spread it out on a clean cloth to dry. Return it to a bowl and toss through $\frac{1}{4}$ teaspoon salt and 1 tablespoon of the Chermoula Dressing.

Remove the skin and bones from the salmon. Leave the flesh in large chunks and transfer it to a container (it can throw off a lot of oil). Prepare the prawns next by twisting off their heads and peeling off their shells, leaving the small piece of shell on the tail intact. Slit down the back of each prawn with a sharp knife and gently extract the black or orangey red vein running right down the length. Rinse and pat dry with absorbent kitchen paper. Cover and refrigerate until required.

Mix the oil, lime juice, $\frac{1}{4}$ teaspoon of salt and the chillies together in a small bowl. Wash the limes and slice them.

Heat $\frac{1}{2}$ tablespoon of oil in a small frying pan over a medium-high heat. When the oil is hot, add the prawns and cook quickly until they change colour, then turn and cook the second side until pink. Transfer to a plate. Sauté the lime slices in a hot oiled pan until lightly browned.

To assemble the dish, spread the dressed burghul on a large platter. Mound the salmon in the middle. Peel the avocados and extract the stones, then cut the flesh into chunks. Arrange the avocado and prawns around the salmon, (along with a few chunks of stewed pepper – see page 85 – if liked), and drizzle with the chilli oil.

Spoon the dressing over the salmon, garnish with the lime slices and serve.

Chermoula is a classic Moroccan marinade and sauce used mostly with fish. Marinate fish fillets in Chermoula for 2–6 hours, and leave whole fish steeping in the mixture for 24 hours (refrigerated). Serve extra Chermoula with the cooked dish.

If using Chermoula Dressing in a recipe that doesn't already contain chilli, use the chilli powder specified in the ingredients list.

come in the cold

Numb toes, icy breath, 'Old Man Nick' (the harsh south wind) howling at the door. Bring forth bowls of heart-warming sustenance to restore the equilibrium. These dishes do what Mamma's chicken soup does for every Jewish boy or girl – they soothe the soul.

out of

TOE-WARMING DISHES
Soupe au Pistou
Chillied Bean Stack with Sugared Tomatoes
Lentil Soup with Garlic and Parsley Topping
Chickpea Casserole

OLDER THAN THE COUGH
Brown Lentils in Cumin Butter
Italian Lentils with Spicy Sausages

ANGRY PASTA
Penne all'Arrabbiata

BLACK-EYED BEAUTY
Black-eyed Beans with Spinach

GOLDEN YOLKS
Kuku
Eggs Baked with Cumin

FEATHERY FLAKES
Spanakopita

A PROVENÇAL REPAST
Leg of Lamb with Haricot Beans
Haricot Beans

THE RICHES OF PERSIA
Spinach Salad
Burghul Pilaf
Persian Chicken with Fruity Pine Nut Stuffing

WINTER SALADS
Carrot and Pine Nut Salad
Greek Cabbage Salad
Spinach and Bacon Salad
Burghul Salad with Yoghurt, Garlic and Mint

Toe-warming Dishes
Vegetable soup with dollops of pistou perfume the air; dense lentil soup, offering a health-hit with every spoonful; a sizzling hot bean purée with strips of smoky eggplant, chunks of sweet crisp bacon and rounds of fried sugared tomatoes, all doused with a sharpish mint dressing; the humble cabbage, with chickpeas, perked up with ginger – these are dishes to make one sing for supper.

Soupe au Pistou

SERVES 6–8

3 tablespoons olive oil

2 medium onions, chopped

500g (3–4) carrots, peeled and sliced

2 stalks celery, diced

500g (4 medium) tomatoes, peeled, seeded and diced, or
   400g canned Italian tomatoes, mashed

2.5 litres water or chicken stock (see page 59)

300g (4 smallish) new potatoes, peeled and diced

200g (a good handful) green beans, topped and tailed
   and cut into short lengths

200g (2–3) zucchini, cut in half lengthways, then sliced

4 ribs silverbeet, chopped (do not use all the white
   stalk)

salt and freshly ground black pepper

90g small macaroni or pasta shells

fruity olive oil

freshly grated Italian parmesan cheese

Pistou

2 cloves garlic, peeled

1 cup fresh basil leaves

few pinches salt

freshly ground black pepper

3 tablespoons freshly grated Italian parmesan cheese

1 large tomato, skinned, halved, deseeded and diced

3 tablespoons extra virgin olive oil

Warm the olive oil in a large soup pot over a medium heat. Add the onions and sauté until tender, about 10 minutes. Add the carrots and celery and sauté for 10 minutes, then add the fresh or canned tomatoes, stock and potatoes and bring to the boil. Simmer, uncovered, for 10 minutes more.

Add the green beans, zucchini and silverbeet, partially cover with a lid, and continue to cook until all the vegetables are tender, 30 minutes or longer. Season with $1\frac{1}{2}$ teaspoons of salt and some pepper.

Cook the pasta separately and add to the soup just before serving.

While the soup is simmering, make the pistou. Pound garlic, basil, salt and pepper in a mortar, then add half of each of the remaining ingredients. When smooth, work in the last portion of ingredients (there should be some texture to it). If preferred, the pistou can be made in a food processor: blend chopped garlic, basil, salt and pepper then add the parmesan cheese and tomato, and while the machine is running, pour the extra virgin olive oil in through the feed tube.

Remove the soup from the heat and stir in the pistou. Serve at once, topped with a drizzle of fruity olive oil and a sprinkling of parmesan.

This is a delicious Niçoise soup perfumed with a basil and garlic pistou (the Niçoise version of pesto). I prefer the soup after a long cooking, when the vegetables are very tender and the flavours have melded together, but it can be served after about 30 minutes' cooking.

Chillied Bean Stack with Sugared Tomatoes

SERVES 6

Bean Purée

200g small dried white beans (haricot or navy)

1 tablespoon tomato paste

4 tiny dried 'bird's eye' chillies

3 tablespoons extra virgin olive oil

1 large clove garlic, crushed

1 tablespoon finely chopped rosemary

salt

Garlic Pita Breads

125g butter

3 cloves garlic, crushed

6 large pita breads, split in half through the middle to form 12 rounds

Topping

6 Roma plum tomatoes

olive oil

castor sugar

1 teaspoon fresh thyme leaves

salt

freshly ground black pepper

2 medium-large eggplants

300g streaky bacon, derinded

Dressing

$1\frac{1}{2}$ tablespoons balsamic vinegar (or use wine vinegar)

$\frac{1}{4}$ teaspoon salt

freshly ground black pepper to taste

8 tablespoons extra virgin olive oil

1 tablespoon chopped mint

1 tablespoon chopped parsley

Rinse the beans, then soak them in a bowl of cold water for several hours. Drain and transfer to a saucepan. Pour on 1 litre of water and add the tomato paste and 2 whole chillies. Bring to the boil, then turn the heat down and cook at a gentle simmer for about 1 hour, or until tender, partially covered with a lid. Drain the beans, reserving the cooking liquid, then purée them in a food processor, using enough of the reserved cooking liquid to turn them into a purée.

Crush the other dried chillies. Heat the oil in the cleaned saucepan over a medium heat and add the garlic, rosemary and crushed chillies. Sauté for 2–3 minutes. Mix in the bean purée, add $\frac{1}{4}$ teaspoon of salt and blend together; taste and add more salt if required. Set aside to cool. (If making a day ahead, cool, cover and refrigerate, but serve at room temperature, not straight from the fridge.)

Mix the butter and garlic together and spread over the insides of the pita breads. Lay the bread in a roasting tin (cook in batches) and bake until crisp and golden in an oven preheated to 180°C. When cool, store airtight (they can be made 48 hours before required).

Cut the tomatoes into thick slices. Dry on absorbent kitchen paper. Heat a tablespoon of oil in a non-stick frying pan over a high heat. Sprinkle the tomato slices on one side with castor sugar then transfer them to the hot pan, sugared side down. Cook until browned, then turn the tomatoes over. Sprinkle the thyme and a little salt over and grind on a little black pepper.

Slice the eggplants into rounds and oven-bake (see page 36). (This cuts down the richness of the dish.)

Grill the bacon until crisp then cut into large strips. (The bacon can be cooked several hours in advance if required; warm it through in a microwave.)

Finally, make the dressing. Mix the vinegar, salt and pepper together in a small bowl then whisk in the oil. Mix in the herbs.

To assemble, place a pita bread on each plate and top with a mound of bean purée. Arrange the eggplant strips and bacon on top and garnish with the tomatoes. Spoon the dressing over and serve immediately. Encourage everyone to break the pita bread and to use it as a scoop.

Lentil Soup with Garlic and Parsley Topping

SERVES 4–6

1 $\frac{1}{2}$ tablespoons olive oil

1 large onion, finely chopped

1 leek, trimmed, split lengthways, washed well
    and sliced

300g brown or green lentils, picked over and washed

2 carrots, finely diced

2 stalks celery, finely diced

2 bay leaves

1 teaspoon chopped fresh thyme

2 litres chicken stock (see page 59) (or vegetable stock
    or water)

1 $\frac{1}{2}$ teaspoons salt

Topping

1 large clove garlic, very finely chopped

2 tablespoons chopped parsley

1 hard-boiled egg, finely chopped

Put the oil in a large saucepan with the onion and leek. Cook gently for about 12 minutes, until the leek has wilted. Stir in the lentils and add the carrots, celery, bay leaves and thyme.

Pour in the stock and bring to a gentle boil. Partially cover with a lid and cook gently for 1 hour, or until the lentils are soft.

Allow to cool for 10 minutes, discard the bay leaves, then purée half of the soup in a blender or food processor. Combine with the unblended soup, add the salt and bring to the boil again. Ladle into soup bowls and sprinkle the mixed garlic, parsley and egg on top. Serve immediately.

Lentil soup is another of those wonderfully nutritious and restorative soups – you actually feel better as you eat it. But I have to warn you about the colour. It's like, well… sludge really, and there's not a lot you can do about it. The egg yolk, parsley and garlic garnish goes some way towards providing a contrast of colour, and, of course, the warmth brings out the enticing aroma of garlic and fresh chopped parsley. Serve this soup for family meals.

Chickpea Casserole

SERVES 6

225g (1 cup) dried chickpeas, soaked overnight in cold
    water (or use 3 cups canned chickpeas)

2 tablespoons olive oil

1 large onion, finely chopped

1 clove garlic, crushed

1 green pepper (capsicum), deseeded, cored and
    chopped

1 teaspoon ground ginger

$\frac{1}{4}$ teaspoon ground cloves

1 teaspoon salt

freshly ground black pepper to taste

400g can Italian tomatoes, mashed

$\frac{1}{4}$ small cabbage, shredded

$\frac{1}{2}$ cup stock, or a little more if required

Drain the chickpeas, transfer them to a saucepan, cover generously with water and bring to the boil. Boil vigorously for 10 minutes, then drain, rinse and return to the cleaned saucepan. Cover with cold water again, bring back to the boil, then lower the heat. Cook gently until tender (1–3 hours); top up with water from time to time if necessary. When the chickpeas are tender, drain and flick off as many of the loose skins as possible. If using canned chickpeas, drain, rinse well, then drain again.

Heat the oil in a heavy-based casserole and add the onion, garlic and green pepper. Cover with a lid and cook gently until tender, then add the ground ginger and cloves, salt and pepper. Cook for a few minutes more, then tip in the tomatoes.

Cook very gently without a lid for 30 minutes, then add the cabbage, $\frac{1}{2}$ cup stock and the chickpeas and continue cooking, uncovered, until the cabbage is tender; add more stock if necessary. Serve hot.

This is even more delicious the following day and makes a substantial, inexpensive vegetarian main course.

Older Than The Cough
Most lentil dishes look, well, brown. But it's a pity if the look puts you off making them. The roasted-nut, spicy taste of toasted cumin seeds mingling with the earthy flavour of lentils, freshened with a squirt of lemon is quietly stunning, and a dish of lentils cooked with celery and sage and chunks of well-made sausages has plenty of appeal in winter.

Brown Lentils in Cumin Butter

SERVES 4–6

1 large onion, finely chopped

3 tablespoons (about 30g) butter

3 cloves garlic, crushed

2 teaspoons toasted and ground cumin seeds
   (see page 27)

250g (about 1 $\frac{1}{4}$ cups) brown lentils, picked over and
   washed

freshly ground black pepper to taste

$\frac{1}{2}$ teaspoon salt

juice of $\frac{1}{2}$ a lemon

Put the onion in a saucepan with 2 tablespoons of the butter. Cover with a lid and cook very gently for about 10 minutes, or until golden-yellow and soft. Add the garlic and cook for a few minutes more, then blend in the ground cumin. Cook for 1 minute, stirring, then mix in the lentils.

Blend in 600ml water. Bring to the boil, turn heat to very low, cover with a lid and cook for 45 minutes or until tender; the lentils should hold their shape and should not be soupy.

Check that the water doesn't evaporate; add a little hot water if necessary.

Remove the pan from the heat, grind on some pepper and mix in the salt, lemon juice and the last tablespoon of butter. Serve immediately, or cool, cover and refrigerate; the flavours seem to settle in after a day. Reheat to serve.

Italian Lentils with Spicy Sausages

SERVES 4

300g brown lentils (about 1 $\frac{1}{2}$ cups), picked over
   and washed

2 tablespoons olive oil

4 rashers streaky bacon, derinded and finely chopped

1 small onion, finely chopped

1 stick celery, finely chopped

3 cloves garlic, crushed

$\frac{1}{2}$ cup canned Italian tomatoes, mashed

1 tablespoon chopped fresh sage, plus a few sprigs
   to garnish

1 teaspoon salt

freshly ground black pepper to taste

12 spicy sausages, pricked with a fork (use decent
   meaty sausages)

Put the lentils in a saucepan and cover generously with cold water. Bring to the boil, lower the heat and cover with a lid. Cook gently for 15 minutes, then drain.

Put the oil in a large frying pan set over a high heat and when hot put in the bacon. Cook for 5 minutes, then add the onion, celery and garlic and continue cooking for several minutes until soft. Mix in the lentils, add 2 cups water, the tomatoes and sage. Bring to the boil, then simmer with a lid on for 20–30 minutes, or until tender, adding more water if necessary; aim to end up with the lentils intact but moist, not dry. Season with salt and pepper.

Fry or barbecue the sausages, then cut them into chunks and add to the lentils. Cover with a lid and cook gently for 5 minutes. Serve hot, garnished with sprigs of sage.

Angry Pasta An innocent-looking bowl of quill-shaped pasta and its deep red volcanic capping set my heart racing and turned my breath to fire...

Penne all'Arrabbiata

SERVES 6

6 tablespoons extra virgin olive oil

60g piece streaky bacon, cut into thin strips

2 cloves garlic, crushed

2–3 tiny dried 'bird's eye' chillies, crushed

2 x 400g cans Italian tomatoes, mashed

salt

500g penne (quill-shaped pasta)

2 tablespoons freshly grated pecorino romano cheese

a handful of basil leaves

freshly grated Italian parmesan cheese for serving

Put the oil in a medium-sized saucepan and set the pan over a medium heat. When the oil is hot, add the bacon and cook until it is lightly browned. Add the garlic and chillies and cook for a few minutes more until the garlic starts to colour. Carefully add the tomatoes and $\frac{1}{4}$ teaspoon of salt, stir well and bring to the boil. Lower the heat and cook gently for about 35 minutes, or until the sauce is thick and pulpy. The sauce can be prepared 1–2 days in advance to this point if required; cool, cover and refrigerate.

When ready to complete the dish, bring a large saucepan of water to the boil and salt the water well. Drop in the pasta, stir, and cook until al dente.

Bring the sauce to boiling point, then turn off the heat and stir in the pecorino romano and basil leaves. Taste for seasoning.

Meanwhile, drain the pasta, turn into a heated serving bowl and pour the sauce over. Toss gently and serve immediately with parmesan cheese.

Arrabbiata sauce doesn't always contain bacon and it can be omitted if you prefer.

How to...

Enjoy Pecorino Cheese — Pecorino is the name given to Italian cheeses made from sheep's milk. The name after pecorino indicates where the cheese is from, or the style in which it is made. The flavour of the cheese varies according to the pastures the sheep graze on, and whether the curd is cooked during cheesemaking. Most pecorino cheeses can be eaten young and fresh, or aged, and used as a table or a grating cheese.

The recipe for pecorino romano, the most well known of the pecorino cheeses, has remained unchanged for centuries. For this cheese, the curd is cooked and the resulting cheese is aged for around eight months. Once it matures, the flavour is salty, slightly fruity and tangy. It's an essential ingredient in many Roman dishes.

Pecorino sardo (from Sardinia) and pecorino siciliano (from Sicily) are the most pungent varieties, although both are delightful when eaten young and fresh. The curds are not cooked during cheesemaking (they are left unpasteurised) and the cheeses have a higher fat content than that of pecorino romano. Peppercorns are added to pecorino siciliano to make pecorino pepato, a pungent, spicy table cheese.

Pecorino toscano is eaten as a table cheese when it is young. It has a semi-creamy texture, and a delicate tang and delicious lingering, creamy caramel taste. As it ages it changes, becoming more assertive in flavour, but it never matches the pungency of the sardo and siciliano versions.

Black-eyed Beauty A pyramid of black-eyed beans doused with lemon and oil in a crazed pottery bowl, with nothing more than a long loaf of bread, cool wine in an earthenware jug, and a fresh white cheese wrapped in vine leaves, still seeping whey and not yet pungent, and lunch Greek-style is served.

Black-eyed Beans with Spinach

SERVES 6–10

250g black-eyed beans
400g spinach, washed and finely chopped
$\frac{1}{2}$ cup extra virgin olive oil
juice of 1 lemon
2 cloves garlic, crushed
1 teaspoon salt
freshly ground black pepper to taste

Pick over the beans, discarding any stones or damaged beans. Wash the beans under running water, drain, then tip into a saucepan. Pour on $1\frac{1}{4}$ litres of hot water and soak for 2 hours. Bring to a gentle boil, remove any scum, then immediately turn the heat down to a simmer. Cook gently, partially covered with a lid, for 40–60 minutes or until just tender. Add the spinach and cook until it wilts, stirring from time to time. Turn the beans and spinach into a sieve or colander, drain very well, then transfer to a large bowl.

Mix the oil, lemon juice, garlic, salt and pepper in a small bowl, then drizzle over the beans. Toss well then leave to cool. Toss again before serving.

These Greek beans are usually made with silverbeet, but I prefer the lighter colour and delicate flavour of spinach. They always taste better the day after making; store covered and refrigerated but bring to room temperature before serving.

How to...

Cook Pulses — Pulses are the edible seeds of leguminous plants, which include peas, beans and lentils. After drying they can be stored for many months, but are best used within a year of drying. Lentils can be used as they are, requiring only a rinse with water to remove dust, but dried beans and peas need to be soaked in water before cooking to fully hydrate them. Soaking also shortens the cooking time and makes them more digestible. If you live in an area with hard water on tap, it is best to soak the pulses in boiled water. (Boiling the water drives off the calcium carbonate in the steam. Pulses that absorb calcium carbonate take longer to cook.) Using bicarbonate to soften the water is outmoded because it destroys Vitamin B1. However, the old wives' tip of not adding salt until the pulses are tender is worth taking note of – salt hardens the beans and can prevent them from becoming tender.

Golden Yolks The egg, symbol of life, of love. A meal in a minute. A powerhouse of energy. It's all of these things and more – versatile, nutritious, satisfying, tasty...

Kuku

SERVES 8

6 free-range eggs
1 leek, trimmed, washed well and finely chopped
60g spinach, washed and finely chopped (about 1
    well-packed cup finely chopped)
3 spring onions, trimmed and finely chopped
2 tablespoons finely chopped parsley
2 tablespoons mixed finely chopped tarragon or
    lemon thyme
1 tablespoon chopped mint
½ teaspoon salt
freshly ground black pepper to taste
12 fresh walnut halves (optional)
2 tablespoons melted butter

Break the eggs into a bowl and beat with a fork. Add the vegetables and herbs, salt and pepper and walnut halves, if using. Butter a 20cm deep cake tin, line the base with a disk of buttered paper then pour in the mixture. Drizzle a little butter on top.

Bake in an oven preheated to 175°C for about 40 minutes. If the top starts to brown too quickly, loosely drape a piece of aluminium foil over the top. The vegetables should be tender and the egg set with a crust on the bottom. Invert onto a plate. Serve at room temperature.

This is a Persian version of an 'eggah', a flat type of egg cake. It has a surprise ingredient – fresh walnuts – and a mix of herbs, spinach and sweet leeks. Serve it with yoghurt, cut into squares as a nibble, or in wedges for a luncheon dish.

Eggs Baked with Cumin

SERVES 4

3 tablespoons olive oil
1 large clove garlic, crushed
1 large red onion, chopped
200g bacon, derinded and roughly chopped
salt
freshly ground black pepper to taste
½ teaspoon toasted ground cumin seeds (see page 27)
3–4 large tomatoes, skinned and diced, or 400g can
    Italian tomatoes
6 free-range eggs

Put the oil in a frying pan over a low heat, add the garlic and onion and cook gently until soft. Add the bacon, increase the heat to medium and cook until it is crisp.

Add a few pinches of salt, the pepper and cumin, then the tomatoes. (If using canned tomatoes, flick out as many seeds as possible and, in a bowl, mash the tomato flesh, discarding cores.) Cook, uncovered, for 15 minutes, stirring occasionally, then turn into a shallow ovenproof dish.

The recipe can be prepared in advance to this point; cover and refrigerate for up to 24 hours, but bring to room temperature before finishing off cooking.

Make 6 hollows in the vegetable mixture with the back of a spoon. Break the eggs into a dish one by one and lower them into the hollows. Cover the dish with aluminium foil. Bake for 15 minutes in an oven preheated to 170°C, or until the whites are set but the yolks are still runny (or cook to your liking). Remember that the eggs will continue cooking out of the oven, and that the dish is best served immediately.

Feathery Flakes

Spanakopita has fallen from grace because of the many abominations served under the name 'Spinach Pie'. A shame really because a pie of crisp feathery flakes of filo encasing a moist well-seasoned spinach and feta filling doesn't deserve such a black-listing.

Spanakopita

SERVES 8 OR MORE

750g spinach, washed well and coarsely chopped (or
    500g frozen spinach)

6 spring onions, finely sliced

2 tablespoons finely chopped parsley

5 large eggs, lightly beaten

$\frac{1}{2}$ cup freshly grated Italian parmesan

350g feta cheese, finely crumbled

200g ricotta cheese

1 tablespoon finely chopped fresh marjoram
    (or 1 teaspoon dried marjoram, crumbled)

$\frac{1}{4}$ teaspoon freshly grated nutmeg

$\frac{1}{2}$ teaspoon salt

freshly ground black pepper to taste

100g butter, melted

375g filo pastry

2 teaspoons sesame seeds

Put the wet spinach in a very large saucepan with just the clinging water. Cover with a lid and set over a medium heat. Cook until the spinach has wilted. Drain, rinse with plenty of cold water, then leave to cool. If using frozen spinach, thaw according to instructions. By hand, wring out as much moisture from the spinach as possible. Put it in a large bowl with the spring onions and parsley and blend together.

In a separate bowl, lightly beat the eggs with a fork, then add the parmesan, feta and ricotta cheeses. Add marjoram, nutmeg, salt and black pepper. Beat all together, then tip into the spinach mixture; blend well.

Generously butter a large ovenproof dish (approximately 35–40cm long x 25cm wide x 4–5cm deep) in preparation for the pastry. Lay the filo on a clean, dry surface and keep covered with a cloth. Lift one sheet of filo onto a clean, dry surface and brush gently with melted butter. Top with another sheet of filo and repeat the process until 12 sheets are stacked. Gently mould the pile of buttered filo sheets into the baking dish.

Put in the spinach mixture and spread it evenly with a knife. Trim off any bulky bits of filo with scissors. Brush and layer another 12 sheets of filo, then lay them on top of the pie. Mould the pastry into the edges of the dish, then trim off any overhanging pastry.

Brush the top of the pie with melted butter, then lightly score the surface into a diamond pattern, cutting at least 6 deep cuts right through the top layer of pastry to allow steam to escape. Sprinkle the sesame seeds over the top.

Bake in an oven preheated to 190°C for about 40 minutes, or until crisp and a good golden brown. Gently snip off any scorched bits of pastry from the sides, then allow the pie to cool for 10 minutes before serving. Serve hot or warmish.

Leftover Spanakopita reheats very well in a conventional oven, but not in a microwave.

A Provençal Repast A civilized dish of roasted lamb, imbued with garlic and rosemary, served with a bowl of soupy haricot beans, changed our minds. We'd stay another night in Provence...

Leg of Lamb with Haricot Beans

SERVES 6

3 large cloves garlic

1 leg of lamb weighing around 1.2–1.4kg

freshly ground black pepper to taste

knob of butter

salt

1 tablespoon coarsely chopped rosemary

2 tablespoons plain flour

1 $\frac{1}{2}$–2 cups reserved bean broth (see page 112)

knob of butter, 12 cherry tomatoes, chopped parsley,
and a small bunch of fresh herbs to garnish

Cut the garlic into slivers, then make a dozen deep incisions in the meaty parts of the lamb and insert the pieces of garlic. Grind over plenty of black pepper. Heat a large casserole over a medium heat and drop in the butter. Put in the lamb once the butter is foaming, and brown well on all sides. Sprinkle generously with salt, sprinkle the rosemary over, then cover with a lid. Transfer the casserole to an oven preheated to 180°C. Cook for 1 hour.

Remove the casserole from the oven and immediately transfer the lamb to a board; cover loosely with aluminium foil.

Meanwhile, reheat the Haricot Beans (see recipe page 112).

Tilt the casserole dish and scoop off as much fat as possible. Put the casserole over a medium heat and blend in the flour. Pour on about $\frac{3}{4}$ cup of the reserved bean broth and add $\frac{1}{4}$ teaspoon of salt. Blend it in, then add another $\frac{3}{4}$ cup of bean broth, then stir until boiling (add extra bean broth if the gravy is very thick). Cook for a few minutes, taste for seasoning (add more salt if necessary), then transfer to a heated jug.

Slice the lamb and arrange it on a large heated platter. Spoon the Haricot Beans and cherry tomato garnish (see below) around the meat, sprinkle with a little chopped parsley and garnish with the bunch of herbs. Serve immediately.

To make the cherry tomato garnish, heat a knob of butter in a small frying pan over a medium-high heat. Carefully drop in the tomatoes, swirl the pan and fry for 1 minute only (don't over-cook them, or the skins will burst).

Good gravy doesn't come out of a packet – it's made from the residue of roasting meat. Flour is sprinkled on, which absorbs the small amount of fat (90% of fat should be scooped off) and later thickens the mixture, then good stock or vegetable water (in this case, bean broth) is poured in. The trouble is, the floury bits easily turn into lumps, and lumps aren't ever a good feature in gravy. The way to deal with these unwelcome bits is to squash them with a fish slice, as you bring the gravy to the boil, forcing them to soften into the liquid and thicken it, as is their required role.

Haricot Beans

SERVES 6–8

300g haricot beans

1 bay leaf

large sprig of thyme

1 stick celery, cut into short lengths

1 carrot, quartered

1 onion, finely chopped

2 tablespoons olive oil

2 tomatoes, skinned and diced

2 tablespoons extra virgin olive oil

1 teaspoon salt

freshly ground black pepper to taste

2 tablespoons coarsely chopped parsley

Put the beans in a bowl and cover with boiling water. Soak for 2 hours, then drain. Transfer to a saucepan and cover with cold water. Bring to the boil, remove scum, then add the bay leaf and thyme, celery and carrot. Lower the heat, cover with a lid and cook gently for 1 hour or until barely tender. Drain, reserving the cooking liquid (discard the herbs, celery and carrot).

Rinse out the saucepan and put in the onion and olive oil. Cook gently, until tender and lightly golden. Add the diced tomatoes, drained beans, extra virgin olive oil and the salt and black pepper. Add $\frac{1}{4}$ cup of bean broth. (The beans can be prepared a day ahead to this point if required; cool, cover and refrigerate.)

Bring the beans to a gentle boil, lower the heat and cover with a lid. Cook for about 10 minutes, or until piping hot. Remove the lid and mix in most of the parsley. Transfer to a heated bowl or serve alongside the lamb, sprinkled with the rest of the parsley.

It is hard to estimate how long it will take to cook the beans (although these days most haricot beans cook in about an hour), which makes it difficult to co-ordinate the cooking of beans and lamb. I prefer to cook the beans in advance, then it's just a matter of reheating them before serving.

How to...

Skin Tomatoes — *When tomatoes are eaten fresh, as in a salad, there is usually no need to remove the skins, but if they are used in soups, sauces or stews, it is best to do so. The skin tends to separate from the flesh during cooking and float to the surface when it is cooked, looking unappetising and tasting tough. Also, cooked tomato skins are not easily digested.*

The idea is to heat the tomatoes in water so they swell. This makes the skins taut and causes them to burst. Lower the tomatoes into a pan of boiling water and leave for about 10 seconds. Lift out and transfer to a bowl of cold water (this stops them cooking further). If the tomatoes are still hard to peel, repeat the process.

Never remove the skins from tomatoes which are to be baked in the oven as their skins hold them together and they will collapse without it.

The Riches of Persia A plump chicken roasted until glazed and golden, filling the air with exotic fragrances of apricots, prunes, pine nuts, cinnamon and orange...

Spinach Salad

SERVES 6

2 cups plain yoghurt

700g (2 large bunches) spinach

salt

freshly ground black pepper to taste

1 clove garlic, crushed

2 tablespoons chopped parsley

Line a sieve with absorbent kitchen paper and set it over a bowl. Pour in the yoghurt and leave to drain for 1 hour.

Trim the spinach, wash well and chop coarsely. Put it in a large saucepan, sprinkle lightly with salt, cover with a lid and set it on a low to medium heat. Cook for 8–10 minutes, or until wilted and tender, stirring occasionally. Drain and refresh with cold water, then press out as much moisture as possible.

Tip the drained yoghurt into a bowl, add a sprinkling of salt, some black pepper, the garlic and the parsley and beat well. Add the drained spinach and beat to combine. Cover and chill for 1 hour. Pour off any whey, or beat it in, before turning the salad into a serving bowl.

Spinach has an affinity with yoghurt. This dish, which is more like a 'cream' (although not rich) than a traditional salad, is tart and tasty and makes a perfect foil for the rich chicken dish. It is best eaten within 4 hours of making as the spinach starts discolouring if kept longer.

Burghul Pilaf

SERVES 6–8

300g (1 $\frac{3}{4}$ cups) coarse burghul

1 large onion, chopped

50g butter

3 cups chicken stock (see page 59) or water

$\frac{1}{4}$ teaspoon salt

Put the burghul in a fine sieve and rinse under running water. Drain for 5 minutes. Put the onion and butter in a saucepan, cover with a lid and set on a lowish heat. Cook until soft and lightly golden. Tip in the burghul, stir for 1–2 minutes, then add the stock and salt. Bring to the boil, lower the heat, cover with a lid and cook very gently for 15 minutes. Stir, then put the lid on again and leave to plump for 15 minutes.

Persian Chicken with Fruity Pine Nut Stuffing

SERVES 6

150g dried apricots

75g soft, pitted prunes

1 small onion, finely chopped

3 tablespoons butter

$\frac{1}{4}$ cup pine nuts

1 teaspoon ground cinnamon

grating of nutmeg

freshly ground black pepper to taste

salt

zest of 1 orange (squeeze the juice and reserve for the
   gravy or 'jus')

1 tart apple (something like a Granny Smith), peeled
   and diced

1 chicken, about 1.4kg

1 teaspoon light oil

Soak the apricots and prunes in $1\frac{1}{2}$ cups hot water for 30 minutes.

Put the onion in a frying pan with 2 tablespoons of butter. Cook gently until soft and pale gold in colour. Add the pine nuts, cinnamon, nutmeg, black pepper and $\frac{1}{4}$ teaspoon of salt and cook for a further 2 minutes.

Meanwhile, drain the apricots and prunes and chop finely. Add to the frying pan along with the orange zest and diced apple. Cook for another 3–4 minutes, stirring occasionally, then remove from the heat and allow to cool.

Rinse the inside of the chicken, then pat dry with absorbent kitchen paper. Sprinkle inside the cavity with salt, then stuff with the fruit mixture. Truss the chicken with string (stitch the skin of the cavity and tie the legs together). Heat a large heavy-based casserole over a low to medium heat and drop in the last tablespoon of butter and the light oil. Put in the chicken, breast facing down, and cook gently until a light golden brown, then turn and cook the sides and then the back (keep the temperature low or the butter will burn).

With the chicken breast uppermost, transfer the casserole to an oven preheated to 180°C and cook for approximately $1\frac{1}{2}$ hours, basting often, or until cooked through. If the juices start to catch, add 1–2 tablespoons of water (remove any sediment that forms on the bottom of the casserole dish – it is usually the result of stuffing juices sneaking out of the cavity and caramelising; if you leave them, they'll burn).

When the chicken is cooked, transfer it to a plate. Tilt the casserole and scoop off the fat, then finish off with either a jus or a gravy, as below.

To make a jus, add the juice of an orange, grind over some black pepper and sprinkle with salt. Set the casserole back on the heat and bring to the boil. Bubble up for 2–3 minutes, then pour over the carved chicken.

To make conventional gravy (not traditional, but nice for a change), set the casserole back on the heat and stir in $1\frac{1}{2}$ tablespoons of plain flour. Pour on 300mls of stock or vegetable water and the juice of an orange. Stir until boiling, loosening any sediment from the bottom of the casserole. Season with salt, lower the heat and cook gently for 1–2 minutes more. Taste, and adjust seasoning if necessary. Pour into a heated jug or gravy boat and serve immediately with Spinach Salad and Burghul Pilaf (see page 113). Carve the chicken at the table and serve with the stuffing. For extra information on making gravy, see page 111.

Winter Salads Carrots and cabbage must be the two most boring vegetables. Wrong! Pep them up with chilli, garlic, olives, lemon, pine nuts... And spinach? Dress young leaves with olive oil and tarragon vinegar, sharpen with capers and drape with rashers of sweet crisp bacon and watch it disappear. Whip yoghurt and garlic into burghul and marvel at how it softens into an exquisite cream...

Carrot and Pine Nut Salad

SERVES 6

1 cup plain yoghurt
4 young slender carrots, grated
1 large clove garlic, crushed
2 tablespoons lemon juice
1 hot red chilli, deseeded and finely chopped (optional)
salt
$\frac{1}{4}$ cup sultanas
2 tablespoons finely chopped mint, plus a few sprigs
   to garnish
$\frac{1}{4}$ cup pine nuts

If the yoghurt is very runny, drain it before use. Line a sieve with absorbent kitchen paper and set it over a bowl. Pour in the yoghurt and leave to drain for 1 hour.

Mix the carrots in a bowl with the garlic, lemon juice, chopped chilli (if using), and a few pinches of salt. Cover and chill.

Carefully turn the yoghurt into a clean bowl, peeling off the paper. Beat the yoghurt with the sultanas and mint, then cover and chill.

Heat a small, well-oiled pan and toast the pine nuts until golden.

When ready to serve, turn the carrot mixture into a shallow dish and spoon the yoghurt over it. Scatter the pine nuts over the top, garnish with mint and serve.

Greek Cabbage Salad

SERVES 8

$\frac{1}{2}$ small cabbage, cored and finely slivered (discard
   outer leaves)
2 carrots, grated (choose freshly dug carrots, not old or
   woody ones)
$\frac{1}{2}$ green pepper (capsicum), cored, deseeded and
   finely diced
$\frac{1}{4}$ cup pimiento-stuffed green olives, drained and halved
1 large clove garlic, crushed
1 $\frac{1}{2}$ tablespoons lemon juice, or to taste
$\frac{1}{2}$ teaspoon salt
freshly ground black pepper to taste
4 tablespoons extra virgin olive oil

Put the cabbage, carrots, green pepper and olives in a large bowl. Mix the garlic, lemon juice, salt and black pepper in a small bowl and whisk in the oil. Pour over the salad, toss well, then leave for at least 30 minutes before serving.

The salad is even better the day after making.

Spinach and Bacon Salad

SERVES 6–8

1 large bunch (160 g) young spinach leaves

1 large green lettuce

4 radishes, sliced

2 tomatoes, deseeded then diced

150g derinded bacon, grilled until crisp (cook the bacon just before serving the salad)

6 tablespoons extra virgin olive oil

1 $\frac{1}{2}$ tablespoons tarragon vinegar

1 shallot, finely chopped (optional)

1 large clove garlic, crushed

$\frac{1}{2}$ teaspoon Dijon-style mustard

1 tablespoon capers, drained and chopped

$\frac{1}{2}$ teaspoon salt

freshly ground black pepper to taste

1 tablespoon chopped parsley

Trim, wash and dry the spinach and lettuce ahead of time, then transfer to a plastic bag and refrigerate until required.

Tear the greens into bite-sized pieces and put them in a large salad bowl with the radishes and tomatoes. Toss lightly. Cut the hot bacon into large chunks.

In a bowl mix together the oil, vinegar, shallot, garlic, mustard, capers, salt, black pepper and parsley. Pour over the salad, toss well, then top with the bacon. Serve immediately.

Burghul Salad with Yoghurt, Garlic and Mint

SERVES 4–6

100g (about $\frac{2}{3}$ cup) fine burghul

1 $\frac{1}{4}$ cups plain yoghurt, plus extra for serving

1 clove garlic, crushed

a few pinches salt

freshly ground black pepper to taste

1 tablespoon chopped mint

sweet paprika

black olives

lemon wedges

Put the burghul in a fine sieve and rinse under running water. Drain for 5 minutes. Pour the yoghurt into a bowl and beat in the garlic, salt, pepper and mint then mix in the burghul. Cover the bowl and leave for 1 hour. Fluff up with a fork and leave for at least 3 hours (overnight is fine; cover and refrigerate).

When ready to serve, transfer the salad to a serving bowl and pour a little plain yoghurt over it. Sieve a little paprika over the top, then garnish with olives and lemon wedges.

Who would have thought that by mixing yoghurt and burghul together you could produce such a sublime salad! Try it with oily or spicy dishes, to balance the richness or to provide freshness, or spread it on pita pockets and stuff in a few cubes of roasted lamb or charred eggplant.

cake & pudding

Cake and pudding.

Two gorgeous words.

Enough said.

PLUMP FRUITS STEEPED IN ROSE WATER
Khoshaf

CHEEKY PEACH TART
Rich Shortcrust Pastry
Peach Tart

A WINTER TART
Glazed Apple Tart

TEETH-TINGLERS
Basbousa
Kadaif
Spicy Yoghurt Cake

STUDDED WITH CLOVES
Greek Shortbread

Plump Fruits Steeped in Rose Water Bowls of exotic fruits and nuts, steeping in syrup, with the heady perfume of rose water and lemon peel...

Khoshaf

SERVES AT LEAST 8

$\frac{1}{2}$ cup soft pitted prunes, halved

$\frac{3}{4}$ cup dried figs, rinsed, destalked and quartered

1 $\frac{3}{4}$ cups dried apricots, rinsed, halved if large

$\frac{1}{2}$ cup plump raisins

4 tablespoons pine nuts

4 tablespoons unsalted peeled pistachio nuts

$\frac{1}{2}$ cup blanched almonds, shredded

$\frac{1}{4}$ cup castor sugar

few strips lemon peel

1 tablespoon rose water

Put the prunes, figs, apricots and raisins in a large glass or china bowl. Add the pine nuts, pistachios, almonds, sugar, lemon peel and rose water. Pour on enough cold water to barely cover, then stir well.

Cover and refrigerate for 48 hours, stirring occasionally. Before serving, remove the lemon peel and stir well.

This exquisite Middle Eastern fruit salad made with dried fruits and perfumed with rose water is excellent as a dessert with Turkish or Greek pastries, or try it for breakfast with yoghurt (it's an excellent source of calcium and nutrients). Remember to start it 48 hours before required and use it within 5 days of making.

How to...

Use Pine Nuts — Pine nuts are the kernels from the stone (or umbrella) pine. The small, creamy coloured kernels are found in the cones. When they are fresh, they smell sweet and aromatic, and have a nutty, creamy taste. They are used whole in sweet and savoury dishes. Buy them in small quantities and store them in a container in the freezer; they quickly turn rancid. Pine nuts are more expensive than other nuts because they are difficult to harvest. They require a period of drying during which time the cones ripen and reveal the nuts.

Khoshaf

Cheeky Peach Tart
Summertime. Peaches dripping sweet juice down your arms as you eat. When you tire of them as a fruit, casually arrange peach slices in crisp pastry – so simple, so stunning.

Rich Shortcrust Pastry

225g plain flour
pinch of salt
170g butter, softened and pliable but not oily
1 egg yolk
3–4 tablespoons ice-cold water (put the water to chill in the freezer)

Sift the flour with the salt into a large mixing bowl. Cut the butter into large lumps and drop it into the flour. Using 2 knives, cut the butter through the flour until the pieces of butter are like small marbles. Use your fingertips to rub the butter into the flour until the mixture resembles coarse breadcrumbs.

Mix the egg yolk and water together and add it all at once to the flour mixture (use 3 tablespoons of water to begin with; if the pastry seems a little dry and flaky during mixing, sprinkle the extra water onto the dry flakes). Stir with a knife to combine. Lightly knead with the hands and turn out onto a cool, dry, lightly floured surface. Knead briefly until smooth. Wrap in plastic food wrap and refrigerate for 30 minutes (this is important – it allows the fat to cool and firm, which will prevent sticking during rolling out, and it relaxes the gluten in the flour, which will help minimize shrinkage).

Roll out thinly, with short rolls, rolling away from your body. Occasionally, flour the rolling pin and the board underneath the pastry to prevent sticking. Cut and shape as required.

To bake blind, line into a flan ring and chill until very firm. Prick the base with a fine skewer, then line with crumpled tissue paper and dry rice or beans. Bake for 15 minutes in an oven preheated to 180°C. Either carry on with the recipe, or in the case of the recipe for Peach Tart (see opposite), remove the flan from the oven, lift off the rice or beans and paper, return the flan to the oven and cook for 10–15 minutes more, or until golden and cooked. If the pastry puffs up during baking, prick it with a skewer again. Remove from the oven, and slide onto a cooling rack.

Peach Tart

SERVES 8

1 x fluted 22–24cm loose-bottomed flan ring, lined with rich shortcrust pastry (see opposite) and baked blind (see page 126)
1 cup apricot glaze (see page 126)
juice of 1 large lemon
800–900g fresh, just-ripe peaches (or 700g nectarines)

Bake the pastry blind and brush the inside of the pastry case with a little hot apricot glaze while it is still warm.

Put the lemon juice in a large bowl. Peel the peaches, then cut them into thin slices, discarding the stones and dropping the sliced fruit into the bowl as it is prepared. Gently toss the peach slices in the lemon juice, then cover until required (the peaches can be prepared 15–30 minutes before finishing off the flan). If using nectarines, wash but don't peel them, and prepare as described.

When ready to finish off the flan, drain the peaches or nectarines in a sieve and reheat the apricot glaze. Arrange the peach or nectarine slices in the baked pastry case, then brush generously with the rest of the hot glaze. Leave to set for approximately 30 minutes before serving.

The flan can be prepared up to 3 hours before serving, but the fruit must be very well drained before arranging in the pastry case to ensure it doesn't make the pastry soggy.

A Winter Tart Rustic apple tarts, shiny and glazed under the grill, were cooling on the bench, filling the kitchen with irresistible sweet apple scents...

Glazed Apple Tart

SERVES 6–8

23–25cm flan ring, lined with rich shortcrust pastry
   (see page 124), baked blind (see opposite)
3 large egg yolks
¾ cup crème fraîche or cream
⅓ cup castor sugar (or use vanilla-flavoured
   castor sugar)
800g (about 5 large) cooking apples (Ballarats or
   Granny Smiths are excellent)
apricot glaze (see opposite)

Prepare, chill and bake the pastry case blind for 15 minutes only.

Put the egg yolks in a large bowl and beat with a small whisk. Beat in the crème fraîche or cream and 3 tablespoons of the sugar. Peel the apples, cut them in half and remove the cores. Slice the apples thinly and put them in the pastry case, neatly arranged if preferred, then pour the custard over them. Sprinkle the rest of the sugar over the top.

Bake the flan for 25–30 minutes more in an oven preheated to 180°C, or until the pastry is golden and the apples are browned and lightly charred in some places. Remove from the oven and cool for 10 minutes.

Slip the tart out of the flan ring (if cooked in a dish, leave it in the dish). Brush the apples and pastry rim with hot apricot glaze, then leave the tart to cool completely before serving.

Although the tart is best eaten the day it is made, any leftovers are quite acceptable the following day. If you want to do some advance preparation for the tart, make the pastry a day ahead (or freeze it) and keep it wrapped and refrigerated, but bake it on the day as described.

Apricot Glaze

Choose a small, inexpensive jar of apricot jam. Heat the jam in a saucepan with 1 tablespoon of lemon juice. Bring to the boil, stirring, then pass it through a metal sieve. Discard any lumps – it should drop from the spoon while hot and it should leave the spoon coated evenly and thinly. If it is too thick, thin it down with a little water; if it is too thin, return it to the saucepan and reduce it over a high heat. When ready to use the glaze, reheat it to boiling point and use it while it is very hot.

How to...

Bake Blind — *To bake blind, the pastry is first lined with paper and filled with baking beans, then baked. I use tissue paper, well crinkled, because it moulds easily into the pastry and stays soft, making it easy to remove and posing less chance of damaging the pastry as it is removed. Pasta shapes, rice or dried beans can be used to weight the pastry down; cool after use and store airtight.*

When to ...

Use A Flan Ring — *A flan ring placed on a baking tray produces a crisper base to pastry, as any moisture can freely run out from underneath the flan ring and evaporate. In a flan dish, the moisture is trapped in the dish, underneath the pastry, and it can cause the pastry to become soggy.*

Teeth-tinglers Contrast the teeth-tingling sweetness with slugs of thick inky black unsweetened coffee. Somewhere between the two, Nirvana will be found.

Basbousa

SERVES 10 OR MORE

2 cups finely ground semolina

1 cup desiccated coconut

100g ($\frac{1}{2}$ cup) castor sugar

175g butter, melted

1 cup milk

Syrup

1 $\frac{1}{2}$ cups granulated sugar

2 tablespoons lemon juice, strained

Combine the semolina, coconut and castor sugar in a bowl. Make a well in the semolina mixture; mix the melted butter and milk and add to the bowl. Mix until well combined. Pour into a medium-sized, shallow greased dish and bake for 30 minutes in an oven preheated to 175°C until lightly golden.

To make the syrup, follow the instructions in the recipe for Kadaif (see below), using 1 $\frac{1}{2}$ cups of water.

While still hot, cut the Basbousa into rectangles or diamonds and pour the hot syrup over in 3 lots, then allow it to cool. Best served at room temperature or lightly cooled.

Kadaif

SERVES 8

1 $\frac{1}{2}$ tablespoons ground rice

1 tablespoon castor sugar

300ml milk

75ml cream

1 tablespoon orange blossom water

250g konafa or kataifi (available from good delis) pastry

115g butter

Syrup

1 $\frac{1}{2}$ cups granulated sugar

juice of 1 lemon, strained

Mix the rice and sugar together to a smooth paste with $\frac{1}{4}$ cup of the milk. Boil the remaining milk, then slowly add it to the rice mixture, stirring well. Simmer over heat, stirring, for about 10 minutes, until very thick like porridge. Cool completely, then stir in the cream and orange blossom water.

With your fingers, pull out and separate the matted strands of pastry, then pour over the melted butter and completely coat each strand with butter. Spread half the pastry in an ovenproof dish 20cm long x 15cm wide x 5cm deep. Spoon over the cream filling, then cover it with the rest of the pastry. Bake in an oven preheated to 180°C for about 50 minutes, covering loosely with aluminium foil once it is well browned.

Prepare the syrup by slowly dissolving the sugar in 1 $\frac{1}{2}$ cups of water in a clean uncovered pan; stir occasionally to ensure the sugar doesn't settle on the base of the pan. When the sugar is completely dissolved, increase the heat and boil until it is thick enough to coat the back of a spoon. It will reduce by about one-third. Cool, then stir in the lemon juice.

Remove the pastry from the oven and immediately pour the syrup over. Serve hot, cut into squares, or leave it to cool. The pastry will keep well for 2–3 days, covered and refrigerated.

Spicy Yoghurt Cake

SERVES 6–8

flour and butter for the cake tin

225g plain flour

$\frac{1}{4}$ teaspoon salt

$\frac{1}{2}$ teaspoon mixed spice

1 teaspoon ground cinnamon

2 teaspoons baking powder

1 teaspoon bicarbonate of soda

3 eggs, at room temperature

250g brown sugar

150g butter, melted

1 cup plain yoghurt

Topping

50ml cream

70g butter, melted

100g brown sugar

50g desiccated coconut

50g chopped walnuts

Prepare the cake tin first. Brush a round 23cm-diameter cake tin with butter, then put a disk of greaseproof paper on the base. Brush the paper with melted butter, then sprinkle a little flour over the insides of the tin. Tap out the excess flour.

Sift the flour, salt, mixed spice, cinnamon, baking powder and bicarbonate of soda into a large mixing bowl and make a well in the centre.

Whisk the eggs in a separate bowl, then add the sugar. Beat in the melted butter and the yoghurt, then stir this into the dry ingredients. Whisk for 1–2 minutes until smooth, then pour into the tin and smooth the top.

Bake on the centre shelf of an oven preheated to 160°C for 45 minutes, or until the cake feels firmish and is pulling away from the sides of the tin. Leave in the tin for 10 minutes, then turn it out onto a cake rack and leave to cool.

Mix the cream, melted butter and sugar together in a bowl and blend in the coconut and walnuts. Spread over the top of the cake, then place under a hot grill until golden brown. Cool, then serve with lightly whipped cream or yoghurt.

How to...

Thicken Yoghurt — To make yoghurt thick and velvety, like Greek yoghurt, it is necessary to drain off some of the whey.

Line a small sieve with a piece of absorbent kitchen paper or, if straining it for longer than 4 hours, line the bowl with clean muslin. Set the sieve over a bowl. Pour in the yoghurt, cover and leave to drain for at least an hour, but up to 36 hours.

Carefully turn the yoghurt into a clean bowl and use as desired. After an hour the yoghurt will be thicker and sauce-like. After 36 hours it will be very dense and creamy and can be shaped into small 'blobs', dusted with chopped herbs, paprika or ground pepper, drizzled with extra virgin olive oil or walnut oil and served as a fresh cheese. The thickened yoghurt can be mixed with capers, spices, lemon zest, garlic, green peppercorns, gherkins, olives, etc, and used as a dip or sauce.

The whey, which contains worthwhile nutrients, can be used in baking bread, muffins, etc.

Studded with Cloves Start with crushed almonds, whip them into plump mounds, pinch them into turbans, then marching across the kitchen bench they go, begging to be eaten...

Greek Shortbread

MAKES ABOUT 20

225g unsalted butter

3 tablespoons icing sugar, sifted

1 egg yolk, at room temperature

1 tablespoon brandy

70g blanched almonds, lightly toasted and finely
  chopped (or crushed with a rolling pin)

225g plain flour

1 level teaspoon baking powder

whole cloves

70g icing sugar for sifting over cooked shortbread

Melt the butter gently in a small saucepan. Pour into a bowl and chill until set. Lift off the cake of set butter (discard the milky white sediment) and transfer it to a large bowl. Beat for several minutes until soft and white. Mix in the icing sugar, then the egg yolk and brandy. Beat well, then stir in the almonds and sift the flour and baking powder over. Mix with a fork until crumbly, then knead with the hands until smooth.

Break off walnut-sized lumps and roll into balls. Pinch the tops of each twice, making four shallow indentations. Stud the middle of each of the shortbreads with a clove, then transfer to a baking tray lined with baking paper.

Bake for about 20 minutes in an oven preheated to 160°C, or until a pale golden colour (be careful not to over-colour them). Leave them to cool for about 10 minutes on the baking tray. Sift a little icing sugar onto a sheet of greaseproof paper and transfer the shortbreads to this. Sift more icing sugar over the top, then leave to cool. When completely cold, store in an airtight container.

The contrast of melt-in-the-mouth shortbread and toasted crushed almonds in this Greek Shortbread is quite delightful. If you are able to resist eating them, you'll find they improve after a day or two.

Greek Shortbread

Glossary

Aïoli

Garlic mayonnaise. Use fresh young garlic and remove any green sprouts.

Al Dente

Italian cooking term, literally meaning 'to the tooth' (in other words, cooked but still firm to the bite), used to describe perfectly cooked pasta.

Antipasto

Italian word used to describe a group of foods served as an hors d'oeuvre (the plural is antipasti), literally meaning 'before the pasto'.

Balsamic Vinegar

This superior vinegar, a specialty of Modena, is made using a centuries-old technique. The juice of trebbiano grapes is boiled down to a sweet syrup, which is then poured into wooden barrels. It is left for at least 5 years and, in some cases, for many years more. The resulting vinegar is spicy and sweet-sour to taste, and should be used sparingly. The ultimate is Aceto Balsamico Tradizionale. It pays to remember the old adage: 'you get what you pay for' when you buy balsamic vinegar – cheap balsamic vinegars are usually based on caramel.

Basbousa

Type of cake made from semolina and soaked in syrup, served for breakfast or as a dessert.

Bird's Eye Chillies

Small, dried hot chilli peppers. Use whole or crushed.

Burghul – Bulgur

Hulled wheat that is partially cooked by steaming, then dried and finely or coarsely ground.

Capers

Capers packed in salt have a truer caper flavour than those packed in brine or vinegar. Check that the salt is white and not yellowing (yellowing is an indication of age). Wash off loose salt before using, and soak the capers in several changes of warm water for 15–30 minutes or until they lose excess salt. If using capers in brine, drain before using.

Ciabatta

Slipper-shaped loaf of sour dough bread with a holey crumb and a chewy, floury crust.

Coriander

Feathery herb with an oily, grassy, citrus taste. It is also known as cilantro and Chinese parsley. The seeds have an intoxicating lemon fragrance, and are best ground as required because the heady aroma quickly dissipates.

Couscous

Little pellets made from fine semolina. The recipes in this book use instant couscous (available from most supermarkets and delicatessens).

Dried Oregano and Rigani

Pungent and aromatic dried oregano comes from Sicily and rigani from Greece. Available from specialty food stores. Use fresh marjoram as a substitute.

Dukkah

An Egyptian mixture of crushed spices, nuts and seeds used as a dip with pita bread and olive oil.

Eggplant

Don't salt eggplant before cooking unless the eggplant has noticeable greening under the skin.

Filo Pastry

Thin sheets of pastry used in Greek and Turkish dishes. It is easier to work with fresh filo rather than frozen filo. Sometimes spelled fillo and phyllo.

Flour

All flour used in the recipes in this book is high grade plain flour without raising agents.

Haloumi

Salty sheep's milk cheese. Sometimes spelled haloumy. In Cyprus it is flavoured with dried mint and in the Lebanon with black cumin seed.

Kadaif

Sweet dessert of konafa (kataifi) pastry, layered with a creamy rice filling, soaked in syrup.

Khoshaf

A dried fruit and nut salad. The fruit and nuts are steeped in syrup and flavoured with rose water or orange blossom water.

Konafa or Kataifi Pastry

Type of shredded pastry made by pouring batter through a sieve onto a hot griddle. The strands are quickly scooped up before becoming brittle. The soft pastry bundles are turned into a bowl and broken apart gently, and coated in butter before using.

Kuku

Persian name for an eggah, which is more like an egg cake than an omelette. It can be served as a nibble with drinks or as a first or main course.

Meze

Mezze, meze, mezethakia are the Greek, Turkish and Middle Eastern versions of antipasti and tapas, consumed as a nibble with drinks or before the main meal.

Olives

I recommend using firm black olives in the recipes in this book unless otherwise stated. Soft olives cook down to a mush and can darken sauces. Avoid pitted olives as they have less flavour. Drain olives before use.

Orange Flower Water

Distilled from orange blossoms, this liquid is added to fruits and desserts. Use sparingly (it can be sold in a very concentrated form).

Parmesan Cheese

Parmesan cheese (parmigiano-reggiano) has an intoxicating aroma and a spicy flavour with an interesting granular texture. As you eat it the small granular pieces dissolve and burst into flavour on the tongue. Parmigiano-reggiano melts without running, browns well, isn't greasy and doesn't become rubbery. It is quickly digested (even by infants) and low in calories. Buy it in the piece and treble-wrap it in aluminium foil. Grate as required because once grated it quickly loses its aroma and flavour.

Parsley

All parsley used in the recipes in this book is the flat leaf variety, often called Italian parsley. It has a fresh, grassy flavour. Regular parsley can be substituted.

Pesto

Rich, green oily sauce, made with basil, garlic, pine nuts, olive oil and parmesan and Romano cheeses. The best comes from Genova, they say, because the sea air gives the basil particular character.

Picada

Ground mixture usually consisting of garlic, nuts, fried bread and olive oil, used as a base for sauces or to thicken dishes in Catalan cuisine.

Pissaladière

Richly flavoured flan, specialty of Nice, made with onions, olives and anchovies.

Pistou

Provençal equivalent of pesto made by pounding garlic, tomatoes and olive oil together (sometimes with basil and parmesan cheese also) and used to flavour soups. The name is also used for the vegetable soup to which pistou is added.

Preserved Lemons

Lemons preserved in salt will keep for about a year. Rinse off excess salt and discard loose flesh before using the rind to flavour stuffings, sauces, fish and meat dishes.

Prosciutto

This famous ham from Parma (sometimes referred to as Parma ham) is either sold as prosciutto crudo, a raw ham cured by air and salt (not, as is often presumed, by smoking), or prosciutto cotto, a cooked version. In this book, prosciutto refers to the raw cured ham. Prosciutto crudo is sweet and delicate with creamy sweet-tasting fat. It is sliced very thin and eaten as an antipasto component or used in cooked dishes. Substitute thinly sliced ham off the bone if you have to.

Ratatouille

Provençal vegetable stew.

Refreshing

This means to rinse with water. Vegetables are refreshed with a cup or two of cold water after blanching or cooking for any of the following reasons: to halt the cooking process, to remove strong flavours or to help keep the colour. When refreshing pasta or rice, use warm water, as cold water makes the starch tacky.

Romesco

Catalan sauce based on the nyora pepper.

Rose Water

Distilled mixture from rose petals used to flavour sweet dishes. Use sparingly (it can be sold in a very concentrated form).

Saffron

The world's most expensive spice, saffron is made up of orange-gold threads, the stigmas of a crocus, which are hand-harvested one by one. It is dried in the sun or artificially. In Spain the stigmas are toasted over charcoal. The best is rich in colour and highly aromatic, musky, pungent and slightly bitter. It loses its zest on keeping. Store it away from light and in an airtight jar.

Salad Greens

All salad greenery should be washed before use, even if organically grown. I recommend a salad spinner for drying the greens.

Salt

The most indispensable ingredient in the kitchen, salt, when used correctly, is the cook's best friend. It draws out those nuances of flavour which, had the food been left unsalted, may have lain dormant. Compensating for not using salt in the cooking by sprinkling it on the cooked food is not the same. You are likely to taste only salt. Maldon sea salt, from Essex, England, is a superior salt. It's completely natural, has no additives or bitter after-taste and has a less aggressive taste.

Tahini

Thick paste made from sesame meal. Sometimes spelled tahina.

Tomatoes

In salad recipes, choose ripe red tomatoes that have been grown outdoors. For sauces, use plum-shaped Roma tomatoes, which have few seeds and are fleshy; watery tomatoes will take longer to reduce down to a thick sauce. Canned Italian, Greek and Spanish tomatoes should be used in recipes from these countries. It's best to avoid using cherry tomatoes in sauces as they are watery, have too many seeds and are too high in acid content.

Weights and Measures

In New Zealand, South Africa, the USA and in England
1 tablespoon equals 15ml. In Australia, 1 tablespoon equals 20ml.
These variations will not adversely affect the end result, as long as the same spoon
is used consistently, so the proportions are correct.

Grams to Ounces and vice versa

General			Exact		
30g	=	1oz	1oz	=	28.35g
60g	=	2oz	2oz	=	56.70g
90g	=	3oz	3oz	=	85.05g
120g	=	4oz	4oz	=	113.04g
150g	=	5oz	5oz	=	141.08g
180g	=	6oz	6oz	=	170.01g
210g	=	7oz	7oz	=	198.04g
230g	=	8oz	8oz	=	226.08g
260g	=	9oz	9oz	=	255.01g
290g	=	10oz	10oz	=	283.05g
320g	=	11oz	11oz	=	311.08g
350g	=	12oz	12oz	=	340.02g
380g	=	13oz	13oz	=	368.05g
410g	=	14oz	14oz	=	396.09g
440g	=	15oz	15oz	=	425.02g
470g	=	16oz	16oz	=	453.06g

Recipes based on these (International Units) rounded values

Liquid Measurements

25ml	(28.4ml)	=	1fl oz				
150ml	(142ml)	=	5fl oz	=	$\frac{1}{4}$ pint	=	1 gill
275ml	(284ml)	=	10fl oz	=	$\frac{1}{2}$ pint		
425ml	(426ml)	=	15fl oz	=	$\frac{3}{4}$ pint		
575ml	(568ml)	=	20fl oz	=	1 pint		

Spoon Measures

$\frac{1}{4}$ teaspoon	=	1.25ml
$\frac{1}{2}$ teaspoon	=	2.5ml
1 teaspoon	=	5ml
1 tablespoon	=	15ml

In NZ, SA, USA and UK 1 tablespoon = 15ml
In Australia 1 tablespoon = 20ml
1 tablespoon butter equals about 10g

Measurements
cm to approx inches

0.5cm	=	$\frac{1}{4}$"		5cm	=	2"
1.25cm	=	$\frac{1}{2}$"		7.5cm	=	3"
2.5cm	=	1"		10cm	=	4"

Cake Tin Sizes

cm to approx inches

15cm	=	6"		23cm	=	9"
18cm	=	7"		25cm	=	10"
20cm	=	8"				

Alternative names

cake tin	cake/baking pan
capsicum/pepper	sweet bell pepper
coriander	cilantro
cornflour	cornstarch
eggplant	aubergine
essence	extract
frying pan	skillet
grill	broil
hard-boiled egg	hard-cooked egg
icing sugar	confectioner's sugar
king prawns	jumbo shrimps/scampi
kumara	sweet potato
minced meat	ground meat
pawpaw	papaya
rock melon	cantaloupe
seed	pip
spring onion	scallion/green onion
zucchini	courgette

Oven Temperatures

Celsius to Fahrenheit

110°C	225°F	very cool
130°C	250°F	
140°C	275°F	cool
150°C	300°F	
170°C	325°F	warm
180°C	350°F	moderate
190°C	375°F	fairly hot
200°C	400°F	
220°C	425°F	hot
230°C	450°F	very hot
240°C	475°F	

Abbreviations

g	grams
kg	kilogram
mm	millimetre
cm	centimetre
ml	millilitre
°C	degrees Celsius
°F	degrees Fahrenheit

American-Imperial

in	inch
lb	pound
oz	ounce

Index

A big thanks to the two companies who willingly supplied crockery, glassware and other items for the photographs:

Milly's of Ponsonby
Auckland, New Zealand
Tel. 64 9 376-1550

Country Road
Auckland, New Zealand
Tel. 64 9 524-9685